DUCKS IN THE WILD

DUCKS IN THE WILD

Conserving Waterfowl and Their Habitats

PAUL A. JOHNSGARD

PRENTICE HALL GENERAL REFERENCE

New York • London • Toronto • Sydney • Tokyo • Singapore

Prentice Hall General Reference
15 Columbus Circle
New York, NY 10023

Library of Congress Catalog Card Number: 92-21999

ISBN 0-671-85007-5

Originally published in
Canada by Key Porter Books
Limited in 1992.

Design: Tania Craan
Illustrations: Wallace Edwards (pages 29, 83, 113, 132).
All other illustrations are by the author.

Page 1: *Mallards*
Page 2: *Male American Wood Duck*
Page 5: *Black-bellied Whistling Duck duckling*

Typesetting: MacTrix DTP
Printed and bound in Hong Kong
By Book Art Inc., Toronto

10   9   8   7   6   5   4   3   2   1

First Prentice Hall Edition

Contents

Scott Nielsen

Introduction

George K. Peck

Oldsquaw nest

Conservation of the world's wetlands, and the wildlife closely associated with them, has taken on special importance in recent years. Thus, when I was asked to write a book on the ducks of the world, I was intrigued with the possibilities the work presented. However, I wasn't at all certain that one could logically distinguish all the world's "ducks" from the other true waterfowl, the geese and swans, and I also wasn't certain that I should write yet another book on waterfowl.

I soon resolved the first question by deciding that all the duck-like species would have to be considered, including the whistling ducks (which are more closely related to the geese and swans than to true ducks) and the shelducks (which structurally grade into the sheldgeese, the latter merging in turn with the true geese). The second question was much more difficult, because I had already written several books dealing with waterfowl, including a world survey of the entire waterfowl family. Yet only one of my books, *Waterfowl: Their Biology and Natural History*, was primarily directed toward the general reader. It is now nearly three decades old, and its information on rare and endangered species is badly outdated. For these reasons, I agreed to write this book, in the belief that it will fill a useful niche in the waterfowl literature.

In the text I have highlighted the present-day status of threatened and endangered duck species, the dependence of all the world's waterfowl on wetland preservation, and the conservation efforts now occurring around the world. I have also emphasized the natural history and social behavior of ducks rather than providing more esoteric facts, such as the technical aspects of waterfowl anatomy and classification. However, I have added a brief glossary of ornithological terms, a reference list, and a species-identification key to broaden the scope of the book beyond that of a standard "popular" or coffee-table book.

Virtually all species of ducks that exist today are illustrated in this book, either in color photographs or drawings. Distribution maps show breeding or residential ranges. It is hoped that the numerous color plates will be of particular interest to bird-lovers, duck-watchers, and artists. The photographs were generally chosen to illustrate adult birds in breeding plumage, and in those cases where only a single sex is illustrated, they typically show males because they tend to be more distinctively colored. However, the ducks of the world are so diverse in appearance that the necessarily short, simple descriptions used in this book are often inadequate for field or even in-hand identification. Nevertheless, the combined species accounts, the identification guide, and the numerous color plates should resolve nearly all questions of duck identification. The reader is also urged to refer to illustrative sources cited in the Selected References to more fully appreciate the age, sexual, seasonal, and geographic variations that are to be found in ducks.

The vernacular English and scientific names used in this book, as well as the sequential organization of species and larger groupings, generally follow my usage in earlier and more technical writings. Several commonly used alternative names are mentioned in the text and have also been included in the index, since, like their scientific classification, the most appropriate vernacular terminology of the world's waterfowl is still an unsettled issue.

Mallards

 CHAPTER ONE

The Magic of Waterfowl

Thomas Kitchin

ONE OF THE MOST DECISIVE EVENTS OF MY LIFE OCCURRED ON A FALL afternoon in the late 1930s, when I was about eight years old. I was growing up in a small town in eastern North Dakota. It was the worst of the Depression years, and my father regularly went hunting for pheasants to supplement the family larder. I often went along to help flush birds from the weedy cover along the roadsides. Once we were standing along the road after a walk through a nearby draw. Suddenly Dad cocked his head to listen. In the distance I heard a sound like a thousand dogs yelping excitedly. "Those are Snow Geese," said my father, pointing up to the sky, and with those words I was forever captivated. There, in ragged V-formation, was a skein of white birds sprinkled across the zenith. They were the first wild geese I had ever seen, and I strained to watch them until they disappeared from sight.

I have often wondered if my father remembered that incident, which became imprinted on my mind and altered it forever. Since then I have been entranced by the beauty and mystery of waterfowl and have managed to see more than 140 of the world's nearly 150 species. I have tracked down the nesting grounds of the Snow Goose in arctic Canada, watched the courtship of Spectacled Eiders along the coastal tundra of northwestern Alaska, waded through the tropical swamps of Colombia and Jamaica in search of Masked Ducks, climbed the Andean slopes of Bolivia to find Torrent Ducks, and canoed across Australian billabongs to observe the strange Freckled Duck. I have photographed clouds of Egyptian Geese and Lesser Flamingos while hiking the barren shorelines of the Rift Valley lakes of Kenya and Tanzania, occasionally breaking through the surface pan to sink knee-deep into a quicksand-like morass. Near Wyoming's towering Teton peaks, I have filmed nesting Trumpeter Swans and watched a mother Common Merganser carry a brood on her back while negotiating a swift mountain stream.

Throughout nearly four decades of my life I have never ceased to wonder at the mysteries of waterfowl—from their unerring ability to navigate from the arctic to the tropics and back again, to their wonderful languages of sound and movement, their mastery of the aerial and aquatic environments, and the unending visual delights of their take-offs, flights, and landings. In opposition to former U.S. president Ronald Reagan, who once suggested that if you've seen one redwood, you've seen them all, it is truly fair to say, "After you've seen all the waterfowl, look again, because you have not really observed any of them." Indeed, once you have learned the rudiments of appreciating waterfowl, namely by learning to tell the species apart, you have only barely begun to appreciate them.

If you live near a large lake or the coast, spend a winter day watching the diving ducks. They will be spending much of their time courting. The courtship displays of these species are performed with a kind of wild abandon that exhilarates the observer. Aerial chases are common, with several males closely following the female, sometimes even trying to grasp her tail in flight. In their zeal to displace one another, the males may engage in surface combat, or may resort to submarine tactics, stealthily approaching and attacking their rivals from below, like miniature torpedoes.

If it is summer, there is nothing that can tug at the heartstrings so much as the sight of a family of geese or swans, the male usually taking the lead and the female guarding the rear, with the youngsters clustered together or strung out single-file between. Should a source of danger appear, it is usually the female that leads her brood to safety, while the larger male takes the responsibility for distracting or threatening the intruder. If one is very lucky indeed, it may even be possible to watch a brood of newly hatched young leaving the nest. I have spent many predawn hours at the site of an American Wood Duck nesting hole, hoping (usually in vain) to watch the young tumble down one at a time from their elevated nesting site at their mother's call, their webbed feet fully outstretched and their tiny wings flailing the air. They sometimes bounce off tree branches or bushes on the way down, but somehow always seem to get through this incredible initiation into the world unscathed. They are soon gathered together below the nest hole to follow their mother dutifully toward the nearest water, never to visit their nest site again.

Perhaps the most remarkable scenes involving waterfowl that I have ever experienced were in the South American Andes. There, in the ice-cold streams that pour down from the alpine snow fields and glaciers, one of the most unusual ducks in the world ekes out a precarious existence. The incredibly streamlined Torrent Duck looks as if it had been designed in a wind tunnel. Like a woodpecker, it uses its long, stiffened tail as a prop when standing on slippery rocks and probably as a rudder for maneuvering while swimming underwater. It feeds almost entirely on aquatic insect larvae, which it obtains by diving into the torrential streams and probing with its narrow rubbery-like bill into

Thomas Kitchin

Mallard female and young

the rock crevices of the stream bed. Even one-day-old Torrent Duck ducklings are taken by their parents to the swirling streams cascading down the mountain slopes. The ducklings almost unhesitatingly enter the current behind their parents, and at times are immediately swept downstream. They may be carried a quarter mile or more over a series of rapids and small waterfalls before coming to rest in a stretch of calm water, or until they are able to scramble out to the safety of a large flattened rock in midstream. How the parents are ever able to keep their brood together, let alone raise some of them to fledging age, is a marvel to anyone who has had the good fortune to observe these birds in the wild.

Equally memorable was the summer I spent in Australia, where I went to try to find several rare and little-known species of ducks. These included the Australian Blue-bill and the bizarre Musk Duck, which are diving ducks with long, stiffened tails that place them in the group of ducks called stifftails. The stiffened tail feathers probably serve as underwater rudders, but they can also be cocked vertically above the back during courtship displays. In the case of the Musk Duck, the male carries his displays to the extreme. He not only cocks his tail until the feathers touch his back and inflates special pouches in his throat, but a black lobe that hangs from the base of the bill is also engorged, making the bird resemble some prehistoric reptile when seen at any distance. This posture, and the male's associated loud whistles and splashing sounds, serve to attract pre-nesting females, and may help to ward off less dominant males from the displaying bird's territory. Curiously, they seem to attract non-displaying males, which may approach as close as they dare to the displaying bird, and perhaps thereby gain some chance of sidetracking a female's attention while the dominant male is preoccupied with his display activities.

Closer to home, I return each spring to the Platte River in a kind of annual pilgrimage to rekindle my sagging spirits after a long Nebraska winter. As I leave my home in early March and drive the hundred-odd miles to the Platte Valley in east-central Nebraska, I glance at the dirty snow in the ditches and the still-dead fields of last year's corn and milo. Here and there a small cloud of blackbirds undulates around a field or disappears toward the north, a taste of the great migrations that will soon fill the Nebraska skies. I know that within a mile of reaching the Platte River I will be able to see the traceries of ducks, geese, and Sandhill Cranes along the horizon. I slow down, turn off the radio, and in spite of the cold weather open my car window slightly, to listen for a more ancient and celestial music, that of wild birds.

As I cross the bridge over the first of the Platte's several broad and usually shallow channels, I note with pleasure that they are mostly ice-free, at least enough to provide safety for roosting waterfowl and cranes. These birds seek out areas of open water where coyotes cannot make nocturnal raids and where shallow backwater stretches allow them to doze without being swept downstream. I turn off the Interstate at the first exit and head for the nearest gravel road that parallels the river, watching for waterfowl and cranes feeding in the nearby fields or tumbling out of the sky in near free-fall flight to land in them.

There are usually two species of geese that migrate abundantly through the central Platte Valley, Greater White-fronted and Canada Geese, which collectively might number close to half a million birds. The Canadas are an assortment of sizes, ranging from tiny arctic-breeding races no larger than Mallards to the regal "Giant" Canada Geese that outweigh the smallest race four- or fivefold. The sonorous calls of the largest geese nearly drown out the yelping notes of the small ones, and all blend with the laughing screams of the White-fronts and the rolling, whooping calls of the cranes. It is a wild, exciting scene, and best experienced by lying flat in the tall grasses that grow along the riverbank, with your eyes directed upward, simply waiting for the sky to be punctuated with long lines of geese and cranes. By lying very still I can occasionally catch by surprise a Common Merganser or two floating downstream in a fast channel, or hear a beaver strike the water with its tail as it suddenly becomes aware of my presence.

If the Platte Valley is exciting in early March, the Missouri Valley separating southeastern Nebraska from Iowa and Missouri is overpowering. Nearly a million Snow Geese push northward then, assembling in the valley from wintering areas ranging from southern Missouri south to the Gulf of Mexico. They sometimes form up in single flocks of 100,000 to 200,000 birds, transforming the sky into a feathered blizzard. With the first break in winter weather I head my car east, straining my eyes in the pale dawn light to see the long lines of geese that I know will be streaming north through the entire central Missouri River valley, from Squaw Creek National Wildlife Refuge near the Missouri and Kansas border to the vicinity of DeSoto Bend National Wildlife Refuge north of Omaha–Council Bluffs. On these days I relive my youth, remembering otherwise forgotten North Dakota winters by whether I was able to be at the proper rendezvous to meet the Snow Geese and celebrate the annual spring renewal of life with them.

The Snow Geese flocks in spring are filled with an almost palpable sense of urgency. Should a single bird suddenly take flight in alarm the entire flock is likely to follow, causing the whole surface of the marsh to seemingly lift in unison, amid a din that eclipses that made by a massive crowd at an athletic event. As the birds circle the water, they sparkle like gigantic snowflakes in the sky, their plumage alternately flashing and becoming subdued as they turn into and away from the sun. Then, satisfied that all is well, they tumble back into the marsh, the last birds side-slipping downward to join their compatriots already on the water. Here and there an American Bald Eagle perches in a tall cottonwood or stands on a floating chunk of ice, carefully scanning the incoming and outgoing flocks for any individuals that take flight with difficulty or lag behind the others. Such birds are generally unable to live for long. Scattered piles of white feathers around the marsh are mute testimony to the dreadful efficiency with which eagles keep the flocks culled of any birds unlikely to survive the long flight to the arctic breeding grounds or unlikely to compete effectively with the others for precious space in the nesting colony once there.

One need not travel to the Andes, to the Alaskan tundra, or to the outback of Australia to learn new and wonderful things about waterfowl; there are unanswered questions regarding even such common birds as Mallards and Northern Pintails. What advantage, for example, are the curved central tail feathers of male Mallards or the long and pointed ones of Northern Pintails? Would their removal reduce the chances of a male attracting or holding a mate? And what is the real function of the white-bordered purple speculum (wing patch) in a female Mallard? She does not use it in courtship preening display as does the male, yet it is equally well developed. Certainly, when leading very small ducklings, the female's wings usually droop slightly, so that the contrasting pattern is visible to the young as they tag along behind her. Is this an important signal to the young, and if so, would they be able to follow less well if it were obscured or lacking? Or is the pattern perhaps important during the male's aerial chases of the female, providing him with certain evidence that it is a Mallard rather than a Shoveler, Gadwall, or Northern Pintail that he is so frantically pursuing?

It is not even necessary to pose a question to appreciate waterfowl; it is necessary only to immerse yourself in their world and become at one with them. Remember that their sensory world is not the same as ours; it has different parameters of time and sound and imagery. Birds can respond to levels and durations of light and sound that far surpass our own abilities and understanding, and they probably can see details of their environment with a degree of precision and clarity that we cannot imagine. Waterfowl were doubtlessly traversing the boundaries of North America and Eurasia, and probably transmitting the details of their migrations from one generation to the next, at a time when our knowledge of the world's geography was limited to the view provided from a nearby tree or hilltop, and our communication consisted of babbling gibberish. Even our vaunted modern mechanical navigation systems are incapable of matching those of hundreds of migratory bird species, and we are still often unable to communicate with all the members of our own species without resorting to primitive hand and arm gestures. All too often we kill one another with only the slightest provocation, such as defending our personal honor or our country, and in the past we have sought out and slaughtered entire species of wholly defenseless animals for perceived "sport." We have a great deal to learn from the other creatures that share this planet with us, and the usually gentle and invariably graceful waterfowl are perfect teachers.

Blue Duck

CHAPTER TWO

Extinct and Endangered Ducks

ACH TIME I GO BACK TO WYOMING'S GRAND TETON NATIONAL PARK, A hundred semi-forgotten but wonderful scenes flood my mind and restore my dusty memories to a new brilliance. Recently I returned in late spring, after a lapse of several years, to again see its spectacular waterfowl, especially the Trumpeter Swans. These enormous swans were considered a threatened species until recently, and indeed were once believed to be close to extinction. However, major conservation efforts in both Canada and the United States, and the discovery of a large and thriving Alaskan breeding population, now estimated at more than 13,000 birds, have allowed authorities to remove this bird from the list of endangered and threatened species of North America.

Trumpeter Swans lend an air of majesty and elegance to any pond or lake. In Grand Teton National Park about half a dozen pairs have traditionally nested on a variety of secluded beaver ponds that lie in the shadow of the great range of mountains to the west. When I was preparing a study of the swans, cranes and other birds of the Teton area in the mid-1970s, I spent two summers doing fieldwork in the park. Almost every early morning and late afternoon I would go up to Christian Pond to visit the resident pair of Trumpeters, which had been nesting there every year since at least the late 1950s. As the morning mists began to rise, the snow-white birds would gradually appear, like ethereal visitors from a more beautiful planet.

By late May the female would already be incubating on a nest built by the pair from piled-up reeds, or placed on the top of a muskrat house, while the male would be patrolling their territory, which consists of the entire pond. By late June the nest would hatch, and thereafter the family became a closely knit unit. Sadly, most years only one or two, or sometimes none, of the cygnets survived their nearly three-month-long fledging period, for reasons that I was never able to determine. This poor reproductive success is apparently typical of all the Trumpeter Swans nesting in the Yellowstone–Grand Teton ecosystem. I finally was led to believe that it was perhaps a climatic, rather than biological, factor that

Bill Johnson

was causing the mortality, such as below-freezing night-time temperatures chilling the newly hatched cygnets. Indeed, in recent years the Wyoming Trumpeter Swan breeding flock has markedly declined, at least in part as a result of winter exposure and starvation, and in 1991 only a single pair nested in all of Wyoming.

The decline and near-extinction of many of the world's bird species is an all-too-familiar story, with variations on the theme evident on every continent. In the case of waterfowl, the most common probable cause of population reduction has been the destruction and deterioration of the wetland habitat. Other human effects, such as the introduction of competing or predatory species, and illegal or inadequately controlled hunting, have generally been of secondary importance. At least four species of waterfowl have become extinct in modern times—the Crested Shelduck of eastern Asia, the North American Labrador Duck, the Pink-headed Duck of northern India, and the Auckland Islands Merganser. Several subspecies (the South Pacific Rennell Island race of the Gray Teal, the similarly isolated Washington Island race of the Gadwall, and the Colombian race of the Brown Pintail) have also become extinct, and several other species or subspecies are hanging on by very thin threads. It is worth mentioning these species briefly to provide clues as to how the extinct birds ceased to exist and perhaps learn what might be done to help preserve the currently endangered types.

The Crested Shelduck (*Tadorna cristata*), one of the most mysterious species of apparently extinct birds, is represented in museums by only three preserved specimens. The first specimen, a female, was obtained near Vladivostok in 1877 and was originally believed to be a hybrid between the Ruddy Shelduck and the Falcated Duck. About 30 years later a pair was obtained from Korea, but the female of this pair has subsequently disappeared. A fourth specimen, another female, was collected in Korea in 1916. In 1917 these birds were described as a new species and genus of shelduck by the famous Japanese ornithologist Nagamachi Kuroda. Subsequently, several additional specimens were reportedly shot in Korea, but none was preserved, so only three museum specimens exist, one in Copenhagen and two in Tokyo. Various old Chinese artworks illustrate what appears to be this species, indicating that perhaps it was once much more common. Several unverified sightings of what were believed to be Crested Shelducks have been reported by ornithologists or bird-watchers, even as recently as 1964.

The Labrador Duck (*Camptorhynchus labradorius*) of the Atlantic coast of North America is only presumed to have once nested in Labrador; no nests, eggs, or young of this little sea duck have ever been found. It is almost as mysterious as the Crested Shelduck; however, far more specimens exist, and it was apparently fairly common along the Atlantic coast as recently as the time of J. J. Audubon. Indeed, in 1833 his son John was shown what were reputed to be nests of Labrador Ducks in Labrador, and some dubiously attributable eggs are in a

Dresden museum. The Labrador was a small duck somewhat similar in size, plumage, and shape to the Oldsquaw and the Steller's Eider. The species, which was first described in 1789, may have survived until nearly 1880, although the last known specimen was collected along the Long Island shore in the autumn of 1875. The reasons for its decline and extinction are completely unknown, but it may have had a rather specialized diet, judging from its unusual bill, and perhaps its food base failed at a critical time. Although Labrador Ducks were sometimes shot by sport and market hunters, they were not considered good eating, so hunting probably played no role in the extinction of this species.

The Pink-headed Duck (*Rhodonessa caryophyllacea*) once lived in the many rivers and swamps of India, especially in the area now recognized as Bangladesh. Because the birds were apparently never very common, they may not have been important as game birds, although their astonishing pink heads must have made them attractive trophy birds. It was hunted for the food markets of Calcutta and probably other cities, and was still appearing in such markets early in the twentieth century. The last known sighting of these birds in the wild occurred in the mid-1930s, at about the same time as the last captive individuals died out in England, where they had been brought by aviculturists in the mid-1920s.

The Auckland Islands Merganser (*Mergus australis*) is the last of the species of ducks known to have become extinct in historic times. It was discovered in 1840 during a French voyage to the Auckland Islands, south of New Zealand, but no additional specimens were collected until the 1870s. Later, a total of about two dozen specimens were obtained, the last in 1902, when a pair was shot. Virtually nothing was learned of the bird's biology during this period, although a few families were seen and some young collected. It is possible that introduced omnivorous mammals, such as pigs and rats, may have had serious effects on the mergansers as well as many other native birds, and contributed to their extinction.

In *Birds to Watch*, a recent summary of threatened birds of the world produced by the International Council for Bird Preservation (ICBP), a large number of duck species is included. The only whistling duck on the list is the Cuban Whistling Duck, which is thought to be declining through much of its range. Likewise, the Australian Freckled Duck population was estimated at not more than 19,000 birds as of 1983. This unique species is threatened by illegal shooting and ecological changes in its breeding swamps.

Among perching ducks, the White-winged Wood Duck is now believed to be mainly limited to southern Sumatra, although some birds exist in northeastern India and Thailand. In 1990 it was reported in a forest reserve in Viet Nam, where it had been believed extirpated, and may survive in Bangladesh (last seen in 1981) and in Myanmar.

*The Madagascan Teal (1),
Madagascan White-eye (2),
Brazilian Merganser (3), and
Chinese Merganser (4) are all
endangered species.*

The World Wildlife Fund (WWF), which has been supporting research on this species since 1967, has been concentrating on saving habitats in southern Sumatra, where the largest known population is found. Deforestation, and a consequent decline in the number of suitable nesting holes in large trees, seems to be an important limiting factor.

As to dabbling ducks, two previously widespread Old World species are believed to be in current danger. The once very common Baikal Teal of northeastern Asia has declined greatly in recent years. South Korea has evidently become the most important wintering area of the remaining flocks, with about 19,000 birds observed there in 1987–88. The Marbled Teal's population has also shrunk drastically. Its breeding range is now mostly limited to Morocco, Iraq, and Iran; the once large breeding population in the former USSR is now apparently confined to only three lakes in Azerbaijan. The primary remaining wintering concentrations are in Morocco, Turkey, Iran and Pakistan, countries with governments that do not make a priority of conserving vital wetlands.

Many of the other seriously endangered forms of dabbling ducks are island-dwelling species. These tend to be small populations of limited genetic diversity, and which often suffer from the effects of introduced predators or competitors. The status of the Madagascan Teal is little known, but the bird has not been observed by ornithologists for many years and is probably gravely endangered. The New Zealand race of the Brown Teal now occurs as only relict populations in Fiordland National Park and adjoining sounds in the southwest of the South Island and the north of the North Island (Great Barrier Island of Hauraki Gulf and in Northland). Its population was recently estimated at 2,000 birds, mostly occurring on Great Barrier Island. The North-land population has recently been supplemented by releases of more than 500 captive-raised birds. The Auckland Islands race of the Brown Teal, often considered a distinct species, survives on several isolated islands but numbers only about 600 birds. The virtually flightless Campbell Island race, once thought extinct and often also considered a distinct species, is now limited to tiny Dent Island; it probably numbers only about 30 to 50 birds. The Laysan race of the Mallard (often considered a full species, the Laysan Teal) is limited to, and has become nearly extinct on, that single tiny mid-Pacific atoll. However, its present population is probably stable at about 500 birds. The Hawaiian race of the Mallard numbers about 3,000 birds. Although it is now limited to Kauai, efforts are being made to reintroduce it on Oahu and Hawaii.

Among pochards, the Siberian White-eye (Baer's Pochard) is now apparently rare and declining in its southeastern Siberia breeding range, perhaps because of the effects of rice culture on its breeding habitat and associated increased human disturbance. The Madagascan White-eye is probably in even worse straits, and may be close to extinction, for it has not been sighted since 1970. An expedition sponsored by several conservation agencies spent seven weeks in 1989 searching for this species at Lake Alaotra, without success, as was true of earlier surveys in 1982 and 1988. The ecological deterioration of this lake, from pollution, fishing, and the introduction of exotic fish, makes it unlikely that the Madagascan White-eye can be surviving there. Another pochard, the South American race of the Southern Pochard, is seemingly disappearing from its few remaining known breeding areas, but was not mentioned in *Birds to Watch*.

Two mergansers are known to be extremely rare. The Brazilian Merganser has at times been believed extinct, but has survived in very small numbers and in highly fragmented populations in the Parana River drainage of southern Brazil, Paraguay, and Argentina. The Chinese Merganser is currently threatened by deforestation and associated water pollution in its limited breeding range of eastern Siberia and extreme northeastern China.

Among the stifftail species, the White-headed Duck is probably the rarest. Its total population is estimated at about 15,000 birds, with the vast majority concentrated during winter on a single lake in Turkey, where they have only recently received significant protection. England's Wildfowl and Wetlands Trust, in cooperation with other national and international agencies, is coordinating work on the conservation of this species, whose breeding distribution is now extremely fragmented and whose wetland breeding habitats are quickly disappearing. In western Europe the White-headed Duck is essentially limited as a breeding species to the wetlands of Spain's Andalusian Coto Doñana, a once world-famous wetland that has suffered from water diversion, pesticides, and increasing human disturbance. Although the Colombian race of the Ruddy Duck was not included in *Birds to Watch*, its distribution is apparently highly limited in Colombia. It may still be locally common there, but seems worthy of mention for possible future conservation efforts.

In 1978, Janet Kear and Gwyn Williams produced a list of "waterfowl at risk," based largely on the information in the *Red Data Book* of the International Council for Bird Preservation and the lists of species published in Appendix 1 (Endangered) and Appendix 2 (Vulnerable) of the 1973 Washington Convention on International Trade in Endangered Species of Wild Fauna and Flora (CITES). It is still the most comprehensive summary available. In the case of the numerous island-dwelling forms listed below, introduced predators have most often been the apparent cause of population declines. Habitat destruction, mostly wetland drainage, has been an especially important cause for the declines of species occurring in mainland areas. Other factors, such as uncontrolled hunting and the commercial trade in wild animals, have probably had relatively little effect.

The Kear–Williams list of threatened duck species, excluding presumably already extinct species or races, is as follows:

FRECKLED Duck

WHISTLING DUCKS: Cuban Whistling Duck

PERCHING DUCKS: White-winged Wood Duck
Comb Duck
Mandarin

DABBLING DUCKS: Blue Duck
Madagascan Teal
Rennell Island Teal (race of Gray Teal)
Auckland Islands Teal (race of Brown Teal)
Campbell Island Teal (race of Brown Teal)
New Zealand Teal (race of Brown Teal)
Mexican Duck (race of Mallard)
Hawaiian Duck (race of Mallard)
Laysan Duck (race of Mallard)
Philippine Duck
Galapagos Pintail (race of White-cheeked Pintail)
Kerguelen Pintail (race of Northern Pintail)
Marbled Teal

POCHARDS: Southern Pochard (South American race)
Madagascan White-eye
Banks Island White-eye (race of Australian
White-eye)
New Zealand Scaup

SEA DUCKS: Brazilian Merganser
Chinese Merganser

STIFFTAILS: White-headed Duck

In a newly drafted "Global waterfowl conservation assessment and management plan" compiled by representatives of the Wildfowl and Wetlands Trust and the captive breeding specialist group of the Species Survival Commission (IUCN–World Conservation Union), a major analysis of endangered waterfowl has appeared. Of ten waterfowl judged as "critical" status, five species and five subspecies of ducks were listed including the following: Madagascan Teal and White-eye, White-winged Wood Duck, Brazilian Merganser, and the probably extinct Crested Shelduck. Of the twenty-four "endangered" species and subspecies, the full species (as recognized in this book) included the Cuban and Spotted Whistling Ducks, Philippine Duck, Bronze-winged Duck, Blue Duck, Torrent Duck (all races), and the White-headed Flightless Steamer Duck.

To highlight the species of ducks that are now believed to be threatened or endangered, a small symbol has been included at the start of each respective species account. It illustrates the endangered White-winged Wood Duck and the Brazilian Merganser within a yin-yang symbol, indicative of the two possible futures (survival or extinction) of such species.

WATERFOWL AND WETLAND CONSERVATION

Many of the waterfowl that are in greatest danger of extinction occur either on small islands or in third-world areas, such as Madagascar and South America. In the developing countries conservation efforts are slight or nil. Higher economic priorities exist, even though governments may be destroying their countries' futures by rampant deforestation, wetlands destruction, and uncontrolled wildlife exploitation for food or export sale.

One important international effort at saving endangered species by controlling international trade in them is the Convention on International Trade in Endangered Species of Wild Fauna and Flora, or CITES. This convention, signed in 1973, places strict controls on international trade in live animals and animal products of species considered at risk. By the late 1980s more than 90 countries had become signatories to its provisions. Similarly, the so-called Bonn Convention, or Convention on the Conservation of Migratory Species of Wild Animals, helps to protect birds and other animals that migrate or move across international boundaries. This convention was formalized in 1983, but some countries, including Canada and the United States, have yet to ratify it, largely because of its restrictions on international commercial fisheries.

In the United States the passage of the Endangered Species Preservation Act in 1966, which was followed by a more comprehensive Endangered Species Act in 1973, has done much to identify endangered species and to direct federal restoration efforts toward them. In Canada, the Committee on the Status of Endangered Species in Canada has produced a list comparable to the American endangered species list. In addition, most states and provinces have produced lists of species of regional concern warranting special conservation attention.

In Britain, a great deal of internationally important work has been done on waterfowl conservation and wetland preservation. Much of this was initiated shortly after World War II, when Peter Scott established the Severn Wildfowl Trust (later officially called the Wildfowl Trust, and still later renamed the Wildfowl and Wetlands Trust), a collection of captive waterfowl of the world, along the shoreline of the Severn River in Gloucestershire, in western England. The trust's mandate is to provide public exposure to and education on waterfowl; to promote a captive breeding program, especially of endangered species; and to conduct basic research on waterfowl for conservation purposes. Within a few years the collection became the most comprehensive in the world.

In 1949 the trust received its first Hawaiian Geese or Ne-nes. The Hawaiian Goose was believed to be the world's rarest bird, with only

Brian Milne/First Light

*Pothole area near
Erickson, Manitoba*

about 30 known to exist in the wild. From a nucleus of three birds, the trust bred hundreds of offspring. Releases into the wild began during 1960 on Hawaii and in 1962 on Maui, at which time the mostly captive population of the species surpassed 400 birds. By 1975 the population of Ne-nes exceeded 1,000, of which about 600 were in the wild. Three years later the total number of released birds approached 2,000. Releases continued in the 1980s, but by 1990 the wild population had declined to about 350 birds. The poor survival and reproduction of the released birds has been attributed to various factors, including reduced genetic variability and an inability to survive in the wild as a result of prolonged captive breeding.

In more recent years the trust has turned its avicultural attention to breeding the endangered White-winged Wood Duck and releasing these captive-bred birds into natural habitats in India and Thailand. Additional birds have been produced at Gerald Durrell's Jersey Wildlife Preservation Trust and at various locations in Asia. The trust has also been instrumental in coordinating the monitoring of European water-fowl populations by the International Waterfowl and Wetlands Research Bureau (IWRB) and has recently expanded its interests to include efforts to preserve the world's wetlands.

Although North America has numerous governmental and many private conservation-oriented agencies and organizations, we should not feel smug or secure about the status of our own waterfowl and wetland conservation. The important Prairie Pothole regions of western Canada (the southern portions of Alberta, Saskatchewan, and Manitoba) and the northern plains states (the Dakotas, plus parts of western Minnesota, northwestern Iowa, and eastern Montana) once covered an area of about 150 million acres (60 million ha) in Canada and about 75 million acres (30 million ha) in the United States. About two-thirds of the Canadian portion was still essentially intact in the 1960s, but only about half of the American portion exists. The Prairie Pothole region may have once produced as many as 15 million ducks annually, or about half of the continent's total, and nearly all of the major game species for sport hunters. However, by the 1970s only about a third of that number was being produced, mainly as a result of wetland drainage. In the United States alone, wetlands were vanish-ing at the rate of nearly half a million acres (200 000 ha) a year, includ-ing about 33,000 acres (13 200 ha) of prime prairie wetlands. Much of this drainage was subsidized by the U.S. Department of Agriculture, which was in direct conflict with the Department of Interior's wetland conservation programs. Similarly, in Canada, the Prairie Farm Reha-bilitation Act subsidized drainage, and provincial support in Saskatchewan and Alberta contributed to the rate of wetland losses in those provinces.

Massive purposeful wetlands destruction combined with several recent years of drought in the interior freshwater wetlands of the Prairie Potholes have been major factors in declines of many of North America's most widespread and economically important duck species. By the late 1980s, the total North American duck population probably was lower (at about 40 million birds) than it has been since European settlement began. This massive decline occurred in all six of the major hunted dabbling duck species (Mallard, Northern Pintail, Northern Shoveler, Green-winged Teal, Gadwall, and American Wigeon) and in the two scaups. The Redhead has also undergone major declines since the late 1970s. The Canvasback population, on the other hand, has remained fairly steady in recent years, and the Ring-necked Duck has been one of the few species to show significant increases. The 1991 North American breeding population of Mallards was an estimated 27 percent below the 1955–1990 long-term average, that of Northern Pin-tails was 62 percent below, and that of Blue-winged Teal was 10 percent below. Other species also experienced declines—Redheads were down 26 percent, American Wigeons down 14 percent, Northern Shovelers down 8 percent, and Green-winged Teal down 4 percent. Only the American Black Duck, up 4 percent from a historic low, and the Gadwall, up 22 percent, provided significant single-year improvements among these important game species. Most of the declines in North American waterfowl populations can be directly attributed to losses in wetland habitats.

CURRENT INTERNATIONAL WETLAND CONSERVATION EFFORTS

It was not until after World War II that the ecological value of wetlands became generally recognized by groups beyond the most committed conservation organizations. In 1948 an important beginning occurred; the International Union for the Conservation of Nature established the International Waterfowl and Wetlands Research Bureau (IWRB) to study wetlands and their associated waterbird fauna scientifically, in order to provide an objective basis for their conservation. Some 23 years later another critically important event took place. A Convention on Wetlands of International Importance Especially as Waterfowl Habitat was agreed upon during a meeting of the IWRB in Ramsar, Iran. This convention, now generally known as the Ramsar Convention, established criteria for the ecological ranking of internationally valuable wetlands, based on the number and species of waterbirds that depend upon them. In brief, a wetland is regarded to be of international significance if it supports more than 20,000 waterfowl and shorebirds, or if it holds at least 1 percent of a region's waterbird population. Countries agreeing to abide by this document must identify internationally significant wetlands within their boundaries and take necessary measures for safeguarding their ecological character. These wetlands cannot be subsequently destroyed unless such action has been determined to be in the urgent national interest of the country. In this event, substitute areas must be found.

The Ramsar Convention was not fully in place until 1974. By 1989 more than 50 countries had become signatory members. More than 400 internationally important wetlands had by then been identified and designated as warranting protection. These designated wetlands represent about 70 million wetland acres (28 million ha). In Canada alone 30 wetlands, representing about 32 million acres (13 million ha), were designated. Directories of such wetlands in Central and South America and in Asia have already been published, and others are in preparation.

In 1986 American and Canadian conservation officials signed an internationally important document, the North American Waterfowl Management Plan, which is a 15-year plan to restore duck populations to the levels of the 1970s. This plan focuses on critical areas for breeding, migrating, and wintering birds in both countries. In the important Prairie Potholes region, for example, 3.6 million acres (1.4 million ha) in Canada and 1.1 million acres (440 000 ha) in the United States are targeted for protection and improvement. Canadian ventures also include ones targeted by the Canadian Wildlife Service for Black Ducks, arctic geese, and eastern wetland habitats. Ventures in the United States likewise include additional ones centered on the Atlantic and Gulf coasts, the Central Valley of California, the Lower Mississippi Valley, the Lower Great Lakes, and the St. Lawrence Basin.

In the United States, the federal administration has been attempting to alter the current legally accepted definition of wetlands. Its proposed Clean Water Act federally regulates use of privately controlled wetlands, supposedly to prevent their destruction. However, using the new definition of wetlands proposed by the President's Council on Competitiveness, about 60 million acres (24 million ha) of small wetlands would no longer qualify as wetlands. If approved, these changes would make small wetlands highly vulnerable to uncontrolled destruction or modification by private landowners and potentially reduce national wetland acreage by up to 50 percent. In Nebraska, for example, nearly all the seasonal wetlands in the Platte Valley, which are of enormous value to the midcontinental population of migrating ducks and geese during spring, would no longer be federally protected from drainage. This seemingly insignificant loss would have repercussions well beyond Nebraska. An estimated 30 percent of North America's entire Mallard population uses wetlands in Nebraska's Rainwater Basin and Platte Valley as a spring staging area, as do nearly all of the Greater White-fronted Geese migrating east of the Rocky Mountains.

Policy-makers as well as the public must eventually learn that wetland preservation and restoration, rather than being a wasteful enterprise, has many benefits. Wetlands not only provide important habitats for waterfowl and many other terrestrial and aquatic animal species but, like the tropical rainforests, their associated plants also remove the undesirable "greenhouse-effect" gas carbon dioxide from the air and help generate valuable oxygen. They also prevent serious flood runoff damage and collect, filter and bind soil-runoff pollutants such as excess nitrates, thus preventing their buildup and transport in underground aquifers. Rather than being wastelands, wetlands are the true jewels of our landscapes. They breathe fresh oxygen into our increasingly polluted world and restore the perceptive observer with their ever-changing, ever-fascinating dramas of natural life and death.

Ring-necked Ducks

CHAPTER THREE

Watching Waterfowl

Scott Nielsen

IN THE PAST FEW DECADES, BIRD-WATCHING HAS BECOME ONE OF THE MOST popular outdoor activities. It can be enjoyed at any level of expertise and experience, in any part of the world, and requires nothing more than good eyes and ears, perhaps a pair of binoculars or a telescope, an identification guide, and appropriate outdoor clothing. In the initial stages, simply learning to identify local species is rewarding enough. Soon, however, most people want to know not only what those beautiful creatures *are* but also what they are *doing*.

Ornithologists, like other scientists, are often inclined to dream up fancy terms for what actually are sometimes fairly simple ideas. Yet students of waterfowl behavior have only to learn a few rather straightforward and sometimes even slightly charming terms in order to understand what has been written about the most common species of dabbling ducks. These ducks include the Mallard, Northern Pintail, Green-winged Teal, and Gadwall. All of these widely distributed species have been studied intensively in Europe and North America by numerous ethologists, who have as their classic reference the comparative behavioral studies of Konrad Lorenz, one of the founders of modern ethology, the study of animal behavior.

These studies, originally published in German, were translated into English during the early 1950s. With their publication, terms such as "grunt-whistle" and "head-up-tail-up" entered the ethological lexicon. More importantly for me, reading Lorenz's work quite literally altered my entire life. Until then I had observed waterfowl courtship as an undergraduate bird-watcher with great interest but without any real sense of its evolutionary significance or even any real means of understanding what was actually happening during these elaborate ceremonies. Suddenly I had found a key to understanding the communication system of another group of organisms. My previously rather inefficient and undirected efforts at understanding waterfowl courtship acquired a whole new direction and dimension. Starting with the Mallard, I began in graduate school to examine the pair-forming

Early (left) and late (right) stages of the grunt-whistle (1), head-up-tail-up (2) and down-up (3) displays of the Mallard.

behaviors of as many waterfowl species as was possible, looking for common threads, unique features, emerging evolutionary patterns, and generally trying to probe beneath the surface of waterfowl behavior.

For anyone who is interested in exploring this fascinating avian assortment of visual and acoustic social signals, which have their sometimes all-too-obvious human counterparts in singles bars, dance halls, and university campuses, the Mallard is a perfect "beginner" species. It is generally common, geographically widespread, and easily observed in city parks, zoos, or the wild. Furthermore, it extends its pair-forming period from early fall until late spring. Thus, between about October and May in the Northern Hemisphere, almost anybody can find a convenient place where Mallards are likely to be courting, and need only sit down, perhaps with a telescope or pair of binoculars, to watch and enjoy the show!

One of the first clues to finding "the singles scene" of courting Mallards is the distinctive "inciting" call of the female. The irregularly accented and extended series of inciting *gak* notes are quite different from the usual female quacking calls. Inciting is uttered with a distinctive lateral turning of the female's head to her side, as if she were sweeping something backward with her bill. This posture and call is highly stereotyped or "ritualized" in Mallards. It is used by the female to show her "preference" toward one male and is a major pair-bonding mechanism. In other waterfowl groups, such as shelducks, inciting stimulates the preferred male to threaten or even attack his competitors. In Mallards, inciting most often stimulates the preferred male to swim ahead of the inciting female and to "turn-the-back-of-the-head" toward her. This essentially submissive signal hides his major weapon, the bill, and helps to strengthen the developing pair bond between them.

A second female sexual display is called nod-swimming. The female lowers her head and outstretched neck on the water (in a manner somewhat similar to the female's precopulatory pose) and swims quickly forward among a group of males. This display serves as a powerful stimulus for initiating male displays, probably because nod-swimming is performed only by still unmated females and, unlike inciting, is not directed toward any specific male.

Males that are close to a nod-swimming or inciting female tend to respond with an array of signals. The simpler postures include a repeated lateral head-shaking, a "mock-drinking" movement (a widespread submissive or greeting gesture in waterfowl), a rapid "mock-preening" movement behind the secondary feathers that momentarily exposes the iridescent speculum to the female's view, or a "preliminary shake" that involves rising in the water and performing a general body and head shake. Certainly at least some of these postures must help draw the female's attention to that male, and probably increase the likelihood that she will be watching when he performs one of his major sexual signals.

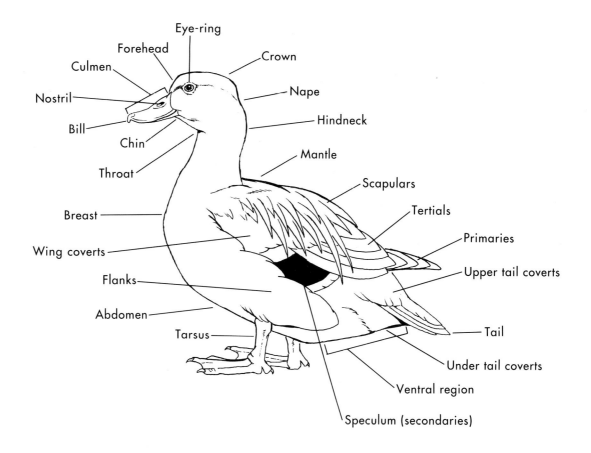

Eye-ring

Forehead

Crown

Culmen

Nape

Nostril

Bill

Hindneck

Chin

Mantle

Throat

Scapulars

Tertials

Breast

Primaries

Wing coverts

Upper tail coverts

Flanks

Abdomen

Tarsus

Tail

Under tail coverts

Ventral region

Speculum (secondaries)

Topography of a typical duck

The primary courtship displays of male Mallards consist of three very different postures, each accompanied by a sharp whistle. The "grunt-whistle" display is evidently a more highly ritualized version of the preliminary shake. The bill is dipped into the water as the head is shaken, causing a small arc of water to be tossed in the direction of the female, immediately followed by a rearing back of the head as the bird again assumes its resting posture. In the "down-up" the bill is suddenly dipped in the water and quickly lifted in what appears to be an exaggerated drinking movement, also causing a series of water drops to be thrown out of the water. The third display, the "head-up-tail-up," is more complex and prolonged. It begins with a sudden vertical lifting of the head, folded wings and tail, which maximally stretches the neck and exposes the wing speculum and the tail area. At the peak of the neck-stretching, a whistle is uttered and the bill is pointed momentarily at the courted female. This is followed immediately by a burst of nod-swimming and finally a turning-of-the-back-of-the-head. Although each of these three major displays is performed at similar rates during a period of social courtship, it is probable that they must serve slightly differing functions and perhaps represent somewhat different "motivations."

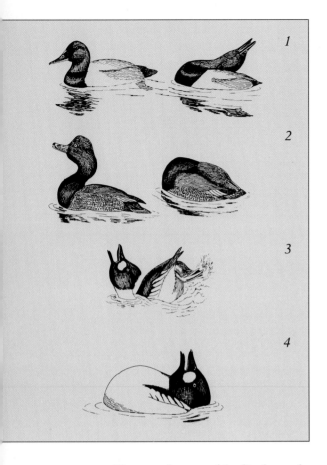

These male courtship displays of pochards show early (left) and late (right) stages of the head-throw of the Canvasback (1) and the Redhead (2), and the head-throw-kick (3) and head-throw (4) of the Common Goldeneye.

After a few hours or days of listening to and watching these strange avian postures, movements, and calls, you will begin to realize that you have begun to decipher another species' language, one that is older than your own and equally rich in nuance and meaning. In the process you will also open the door slightly to understanding the languages of other Mallard-like ducks. Mallard, Northern Pintail, Gadwall, and Green-winged Teal males have similar but yet species-specific assortments of postures and calls that, together with their distinctive male plumage patterns, serve to stimulate mating responses in females, provide a basis for choosing specific mates, and reduce the possibility of mismating among these fairly closely related ducks. All four share two major displays (the grunt-whistle and head-up-tail-up), but the Gadwall sequentially links the head-up-tail-up with the down-up. The Mallard performs the down-up independently of the others, and the Northern Pintail lacks the down-up altogether. The Green-winged Teal normally links the head-up-tail-up with a preceding grunt-whistle. Additionally, males of these and many other duck species perform mock-preening of their highly colorful and species-specific secondary wing feathers, momentarily flashing them toward specific females. The display is so rapidly performed that it has a strong visual "flash-effect," which probably attracts the female's attention and allows the male to follow up quickly with one or more of several more elaborate postures.

It is likely that the various aspects of social courtship in ducks serve quite different functions in the pairing process. The complex male displays performed in a highly competitive situation seem to be closely related to the mate-choosing process. The simpler combination of inciting by the female and a turning-of-the-back-of-the-head toward her by the male, which is a much more prolonged and universal activity among ducks, seems to mold and strengthen the bond between a particular pair. Finally, an entirely different set of signals is associated with copulation, and, like the pair-bonding behavior, these signals exhibit great similarities across rather broad groups of waterfowl.

During spring migration in the Great Plains of North America, one may easily find small groups of Northern Pintails flying in tight formation. Invariably they consist of a single female and from two or three to a dozen or more males. The female leads the chase, uttering a distinctive series of irregular rattling notes. In seemingly frantic efforts to escape, she will make towering climbs, followed by dizzying dives and swerving maneuvers that would put even an expert stunt pilot to shame. The males in turn will stretch their long necks and utter fluty burp-whistles as they jostle for the best position close to the hen. These long courtship flights often last 15 or 20 minutes, apparently until the female begins to tire. She then heads for the water, where a new round of aquatic courtship begins.

Later on during spring migration, "three-bird flights" become more common. The participants are a single pair plus an intruding male.

© John Gerlach/Tom Stack & Associates

Male Black–Mallard hybrid

Frequently the flight begins when a pair flies over the "loafing spot" of a drake whose mate is already sitting on eggs. As the pair flies over, the drake takes off and chases the two for varying distances, seemingly expelling them from his territory. Whether such activities serve for territorial expulsion or reflect the male's continuing sexual interest in females is still debated.

If you observe any of the diving duck species, you will find none of these specific postures typical of the dabbling ducks, although in many some wing-preening displays exist, usually in precopulatory rather than in courtship situations. Diving ducks have markedly different display characteristics, which require separate terminologies and careful study to understand. For example, among the pochards, the typical male courtship displays include "head-throws," rapid tossing movements of the head back toward the tail, accompanied by a call at the point of maximum neck extension. The same call is uttered during a "kinked-neck" posture, where the neck is stretched vertically but the head remains horizontal. Or the male may perform a "sneak" posture, extending his head and neck toward another male in a seemingly threatening manner. In common with dabbling ducks, all of these postures have varied similarities and differences among related species, while the behaviors associated with copulation are more uniform. In

The display shake of the Spectacled Eider (1), the kicks display of the Red-breasted Merganser (2), and the crest-erection of the Hooded Merganser (3).

the case of pochards, alternated drinking and preening movements are the usual precopulatory displays, rather than the mutual vertical head-pumping of dabbling ducks.

The greatest diversity of aquatic courtship displays exists among the sea ducks. In many cases, these typically heavy-bodied birds use spectacular postures and calls rather than aerial displays. For example, Common Goldeneyes are well known for their complex display repertoire. Males have three distinct head-throw displays, as well as several other neck-stretching postures. In the simplest head-throw, the head is quickly tossed back to the rump, and a low, rattling call is uttered before the head is returned to its starting position. Less commonly, a "head-throw-kick" is performed, in either a "fast" or "slow" mode. The kick portion of this display is a sudden thrust backward with both feet, momentarily exposing their yellow webs and throwing a sheet of water back several feet. The head-throw-kick displays probably serve both as sexual signals and as implied threats toward other competing males.

Beyond watching the social behavior of waterfowl, you can engage in other avenues of personal exploration, which can sometimes contribute to our general understanding of waterfowl biology. One of the first indications of the possible genetic effect on American Black Ducks of the expanding range of the Mallard in eastern North America came about as a result of a single interested person's curiosity. During the early 1950s, C. E. Goodwin observed the changing numbers of Mallards, Black Ducks, and their hybrids in park ponds of Toronto and reported his observations in the *Ontario Field Biologist*. A subsequent analysis of Audubon Christmas Count data dating from 1900 confirmed Goodwin's observations and made it possible to track the changes in Mallard and American Black Duck populations throughout eastern North America.

Other enjoyable duck-related activities include joining local environmental groups concerned with preserving waterfowl and their habitats, and becoming involved in nature photography, nature art, or decoy-carving. There are many waterfowl conservation activities that individuals can undertake. One obvious one is to erect nesting boxes in trees or on poles for hole-nesting ducks (mainly American Wood Ducks, Buffleheads, goldeneyes, and mergansers), especially in areas where natural nest sites are in short supply. It has been suggested that the Wood Duck's population recovery during and after the 1940s was enhanced by the availability of nesting boxes, and there seems to be little doubt that the expansion of its nesting range into North America's prairie states and provinces has been accelerated by nest box erection projects. These boxes are sometimes used by squirrels, owls, and other wildlife, and thus each one becomes a kind of surprise package every spring.

Nest boxes suitable for nesting waterfowl are fairly easy and inexpensive to construct. They can be built of thick external plywood or

Wood Duck box

George K. Peck

cedar boards. Depending on the size of the intended duck species, the box should be 15 to 25 inches (40 to 65 cm) deep from the entrance hole placed near the top of the box to the floor, which should be about 10 inches (25 cm) square. An oval entrance hole measuring 3 x 4 inches (8 x 10 cm) is suitable for Wood Ducks, goldeneyes and Hooded Mergansers. A smaller one (about 2.5 inches/6 cm in diameter) is ideal for Buffleheads, while a larger opening (about 4 x 5 inches/10 x 13 cm) is needed for Common Mergansers and Black-bellied Whistling Ducks. The top of the box should be slightly sloping, and hinged to allow periodic cleaning or inspection. A tin lining around or over the entrance hole will help prevent squirrels from enlarging it for their own use and may reduce access by raccoons. Small drainage holes in the floor are needed, and small ventilation holes between the overhanging roof and entrance are desirable. No perch should be provided, as ducks do not use them. The front inside wall of the box should have a roughened surface or, better yet, a wire mesh "ladder" for helping the young to climb out.

The finished box should be placed about 10 to 20 feet (3 to 6 m) above ground, or as high as is practical and appropriate for the local environment. Areas that hold standing water well into the summer are, of course, most desirable. The box should be close to (or even above) standing water, and the entrance hole should be unobstructed by nearby branches. The box should also be tilted slightly forward to help the ducklings leave easily, and suitable safe "landing sites" should be present directly below it. Wire mesh or tin can be placed around the base of the tree in areas where beavers are present, but it is very difficult to keep squirrels and raccoons completely out. Raccoons especially are serious predators, although they rarely can enter houses with holes under 4 inches (10 cm) in diameter or oval holes less than 4 inches high. Some snakes are also very difficult to keep out, as are European Starlings. Placing the box above water, on a narrow metal post equipped with a 20-inch-diameter (50-cm) conical metal shield or galvanized heating duct sleeve, helps discourage raccoons and snakes. Where raccoons are not a problem but starlings are, placing horizontally oriented boxes with large entrance holes in densely timbered sites helps to deter starlings while still attracting some Wood Ducks.

The interior of the box should be fairly dark and left unpainted. Grass, wood shavings (especially cedar, which discourages insects), or other similar materials should be placed on the floor as nesting materials. These materials should be changed each year, early in the spring before the box is occupied. The box should be disturbed as little as possible when it is in use. Once it has been successfully used by a duck, she is likely to return the following year; however, after a nest failure, she might well choose a new site the next year. Often several years may pass before a box receives its maximum use, so patience is required!

Common Goldeneyes

CHAPTER FOUR

Ducks of the World

MOST RECENT CLASSIFICATIONS OF WATERFOWL HAVE SUBDIVIDED THE family into varying numbers of "tribes" of related species. In this chapter, they are represented by ten major subdivisions. Within each tribe, the number of species range from as few as one (in the Freckled Duck and Torrent Duck tribes) to as many as 39 (in the dabbling ducks). Those groups having the greatest number of seemingly primitive traits linking them to geese and swans as well as other ducks are listed first (the whistling ducks and Freckled Duck), and those with the largest number of evidently specialized traits are placed last (the sea ducks and stifftails). Within each tribe, the species are grouped in a linear sequence that reflects their possible interspecies relationships.

Every bird species is known among ornithologists by a two-part Latin name (genus and species), which is printed here in italics, with the generic or general name capitalized and the specific or species name lowercased. A third (subspecific) name may at times be used to designate recognizable geographic races.

The dark areas on the maps indicate breeding or residential ranges.

Scott Nielsen

Whistling Ducks

Wandering Whistling Ducks

M. P. Kahl/VIREO

THE WHISTLING DUCKS OF THE WORLD ARE NEARLY ALL INCLUDED IN A single genus, *Dendrocygna*, which somewhat inappropriately translates as "tree-swan." The name is not altogether inaccurate, for most species are able to perch in trees fairly well, and some even nest in tree cavities. (The collective term "tree ducks" is sometimes applied to the group as well.) Furthermore, the whistling ducks have some anatomical characteristics that seem to link them more closely to the swans and geese than to any of the true ducks. It is possible that they are descendants of a group of ancestral waterfowl that branched off soon after the family emerged, probably from marsh-dwelling birds resembling the modern-day screamers of South America and the semi-aquatic Magpie or Semipalmated Goose of tropical Australia. Like these birds, and in common with geese and swans, their lower legs are covered with a network of polygonal scales, which are not arranged in linear rows. This minor attribute presumably has no value in helping the duck survive, and so has been carried on throughout all these groups without adaptive modification. As such, it is a "conservative" trait that helps to define all the living members of these groups.

Besides this trait, whistling ducks have plumage patterns that are identical in the two sexes and whistling vocalizations that appear to lack obvious sexual differences. Both of these features are related to the fact that, like geese and swans, whistling ducks form strong, possibly permanent, pair bonds, with both sexes participating equally in nesting and brood-rearing responsibilities. In fact, in at least some and perhaps all whistling ducks, the male participates in and in some cases may do most of the incubation. Male incubation behavior is extremely rare among other waterfowl. I have observed it in the White-backed Duck, which, together with a variety of other behavioral traits, helps link this species to the whistling ducks rather than the stiff-tailed ducks, where it has been traditionally placed by waterfowl taxonomists.

Whistling ducks have several other features that distinguish them from all other ducks, including rather short, rounded wings, a long neck, and long legs. These features produce a distinctive in-flight profile, with the feet trailing out behind the tip of the tail, a relatively slow flight speed, and leisurely wingbeats. Calling in flight is also common in these birds, which tend to be quite social and gregarious. The downy young of all whistling ducks, except the White-backed Duck, are distinctively marked with a pale stripe that extends from each eye backward around the nape.

Spotted Whistling Duck

(Dendrocygna guttata)

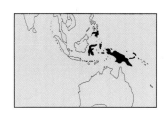

Female Spotted Whistling Duck and brood

Paul Johnsgard

This is the rarest and least known whistling duck. It is limited to a few islands of the Philippines; Sulawesi (Celebes), the Moluccas, and other small Indonesian islands; and New Guinea, including its adjoining islands east to the Bismarck Archipelago. There it occurs in marshes and shallow lakes, especially those having broad grassy margins and tree-lined shores, where it can readily perch on above-water or partly submerged tree branches. The Spotted Whistling Duck nests in hollow trees, but very little is known of its breeding biology. The nesting season in the wild is thought to be quite prolonged and centered on the region's wet season, which begins in the austral spring. In one of the rare cases where this duck has bred in captivity, a pair laid 11 eggs in a wooden enclosure at England's Wildfowl Trust. Evidently both sexes incubated (although this is very difficult to determine because the sexes are identical in appearance), and the chicks hatched in 31 days.

Like all whistling ducks, the strongly patterned chicks are extremely attractive, and are closely attended by their parents. They are fully feathered after about seven weeks, and in less than a year acquire the adult plumage, with its distinctive dark-edged white spotting on the fulvous flanks. The slightly crested head is brown with a darker crown, and the bill is grayish, with pink to reddish tinges near its base. The vanes of the outermost primary feathers are strongly indented, causing them to vibrate and produce a whirring noise during flight. These birds seem to call rather infrequently, producing a double- or four-syllable call, the latter sounding like *whe-a-whew'-whew*.

Spotted Whistling Ducks appear to be surviving well. They live in habitats that are for the most part still not greatly affected by human activities. In addition, they feed on the seeds of various aquatic plants, which are available in abundance, and are apparently not exploited by humans for food.

Plumed Whistling Duck

(Dendrocygna eytoni)

Adult Plumed Whistling Duck

Of all the whistling ducks the Plumed, or Eyton's, Whistling Duck is perhaps the most attractive. It occupies nearly half of the northern and eastern portions of Australia, where it is especially common in tropical grasslands with shallow lagoons edged by meadows and grassy plains. It has no need for trees or swamps, spending its days roosting in flocks while swimming or standing near shore, often in association with Wandering Whistling Ducks. The flocks fly out from swamps toward evening to forage on land, and like many whistling ducks are semi-nocturnal in activity. During the long dry season, they eat mostly grasses and sedges found along the shores, while during the wet season grasses are almost exclusively eaten.

Adult Plumed Whistling Ducks can be easily recognized by the long golden flank plumes, which project from the sides and curve upward over the back in swimming individuals. The sides are vertically barred with rusty brown and black. The bill is yellow to pinkish yellow, with blackish mottling or spots, and the eyes of adults are a distinctive pale yellow. Young birds show a rudimentary development of the long flank plumes and distinctive barring on the sides, but do have spotted bills.

Like many Australian waterfowl, this bird is nomadic, and in rare cases may disperse and move as far as 1,200 miles (1,900 km) from its dry-season refuges to breeding sites. Breeding begins at the onset of the wet season, which usually occurs around the first of the year in northern Australia, with February and March being peak breeding times. It breeds during summer or early autumn in southern Australia.

Nests are simple ground scrapes, usually with a bush or grass for cover, and in common with other whistling ducks the clutches are fairly large, numbering 8 to 14 eggs. Within hours after hatching, the young are led to water, and after fledging, flocks begin to form.

The population of this species is apparently secure. For now its tropical lagoon and grassland habitats are not threatened and may even be increasing, because current grazing activities provide new foraging opportunities for it.

Fulvous Whistling Duck

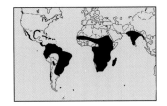

(*Dendrocygna bicolor*)

Adult Fulvous Whistling Duck

Scott Nielsen

This is by far the most widespread of all the whistling ducks. Remarkably, in spite of its multi-continental distribution (North and South America, Africa, and India), this species exhibits no measurable geographic variation. If one accepts that the birds from the Americas have been isolated from those of the Old World for a very long time, the reason for this is hard to imagine. Alternatively, it is possible that the species has greatly extended its geographic distribution in the last few millennia, even though it is a non-migratory bird over most of its range.

The Fulvous Whistling Duck is a grassland-adapted duck, with little or no need for trees for perching or nesting; nesting only rarely occurs in tree cavities or similar natural hollows. Like Plumed Whistling Ducks, its food consists primarily of grass seeds. In North America, it is closely associated with rice culture and feeds heavily on rice in the spring season when water-planted seeds are easily available. The flooded rice also provides perfect nesting cover, especially where it is heavily infested with sedges and broad-leaved weeds.

Although the Fulvous Whistling Duck is similar in appearance to the Wandering Whistling Duck, it can be easily distinguished by several plumage differences. The Fulvous Whistling Duck is generally a lighter cinnamon tone throughout, without any dark mottling on the chest, and the darker crown is distinctly separated from the eyes by a paler brown zone. In the Wandering Whistling Duck the breast is darkly spotted or mottled, and the crown extends down to the eyes. The two species do not overlap in their ranges.

Like the Black-bellied Whistling Duck, this duck lays its eggs in the nests of other ducks, mainly those of its own species but occasionally of other species. As a result, clutch-sizes tend to be rather large, averaging about 13 eggs. As many as 60 or even 100 eggs have been reported from a single dump-nest, but this is uncommon. Incubation lasts 24 to 26 days, and fledging of the young requires seven weeks. Along the Gulf Coast of North America, there is a southward movement into coastal Mexico during the colder months; however, over much of the species' range, little if any seasonal migration seems to occur.

The Fulvous Whistling Duck is very common over most of its original range.

Wandering Whistling Duck

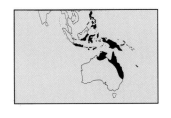

(*Dendrocygna arcuata*)

Adult Wandering Whistling Duck

In southeastern Asia, this species' range takes over not far from where that of the Fulvous Whistling Duck terminates in Myanmar. It ranges from Java, Borneo, and the Philippines southeast to tropical Australia and New Guinea. The two species certainly evolved from a common ancestor. The Wandering Whistling Duck is perhaps more aquatic; it is often called the Water Whistling Duck in Australia, to distinguish it from the Plumed, which is referred to as the Grass Whistling Duck. It forages in water up to about 10 feet (3 m) in depth, diving readily, and, in common with other whistling ducks, often feeds at twilight or even during the night. Seeds and the soft parts of aquatic plants form the major part of its diet, but occasionally considerable quantities of small snails and insect larvae, such as mosquitoes, are consumed. Insects are no doubt an important source of protein, especially during breeding.

In the wild, this species overlaps with the Lesser Whistling Duck. They are easy to tell apart, however. Besides being considerably larger, the Wandering Whistling Duck lacks the definite yellow eye-ring and the contrasting chestnut and generally grayish blue upper wing colorations of the other bird. Instead, it is an almost uniform dark brown on the upperparts and has more definite white flank striping and richer brown flank coloration than does the Lesser.

The breeding season is closely tied to rainfall patterns, at least in northern Australia, with wet periods stimulating breeding and prolonged droughts inhibiting it. Like its close relatives, this species nests on the ground, often under grassy cover some distance from water, and probably both sexes assist in incubation. Little is known of the nesting biology in nature, but eggs of captive birds have hatched in 28 to 30 days. The young are believed to require 12 to 13 weeks to fledge, which seems a remarkably long time for a smallish species such as this. After the breeding season, the birds gather in lagoons, billabongs (river backwaters), and flooded lowlands, with large dry-season concentrations occurring in such locations as the South Alligator River and the Mary and Daly river plains. As the dry season progresses, ever larger concentrations accumulate on the few remaining wetlands. They disperse immediately after the start of the rains, and a new breeding season begins.

This bird is apparently common over most of its original range, but a local population on New Britain Island, Papua New Guinea, is endangered.

Lesser Whistling Duck

(*Dendrocygna javanica*)

Adult Lesser Whistling Duck

The Lesser Whistling Duck is a small tropical species, only about half the weight of the largest of the whistling ducks, the Cuban. Its range extends from Pakistan on the west through India, Indochina, and the Greater Sundas to coastal southeastern China, Hainan Island, Borneo, and Java on the east. Like most other whistling ducks, it is crepuscular to semi-nocturnal, feeding on water plants in fairly shallow water. Flooded rice paddies or lotus-covered ponds and reservoirs are favorite feeding grounds, especially if they are surrounded by trees.

Trees probably offer safe roosting sites. In addition, they are often used for nesting, particularly if they are standing in water and covered by vines, which help to conceal the nest site. Favored nest sites include not only tree cavities or natural tree hollows but also old nests of storks, herons, crows, and other birds, which can be located up to 15 feet (5 m) above the ground. These ducks may also at times nest on the ground under cover provided by thick grass and thorny bushes.

Although little information on clutches in the wild is available, nests with eight to ten eggs are seemingly common, and one nest with 27 eggs was reportedly found, indicating that dump-nesting by two or more females must at times occur. No down is present in the nest, indicating that both sexes probably participate in incubation. (When only the female of a species incubates the eggs, down is used to keep the eggs warm while she is off the nest.) The incubation period is fairly long for such a small duck, probably 27 or 28 days. The fledging period is unreported.

This is a very common species over much of its range, but some marginal populations, such as on Okinawa and the Ryukyu Islands, have perhaps been eliminated. In areas of rice culture, it is considered a pest and sometimes hunted. Over most of its range, however, the Lesser Whistling Duck is probably not seriously influenced by human activities. It may compete to some degree with the larger Fulvous Whistling Duck where their ranges overlap in India, but because it is perhaps more flexible in its foraging behavior the two seem to coexist quite readily.

41

White-faced Whistling Duck

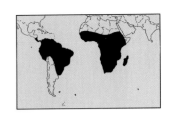

(*Dendrocygna viduata*)

Adult White-faced Whistling Ducks

Scott Nielsen

Perhaps the most visually attractive of all the whistling ducks, this black-headed bird is readily recognized by its white "mask" that extends back to encompass the eyes. It is also uniquely marked with fine black-and-white barring on the flanks, and its underparts are black, which differs from the usual dark-above, light-below combination of colors that provide optimum camouflage. In short, the species is clearly not patterned in a way that helps it blend into its background, as is the Lesser Whistling Duck, for example. Perhaps this species needs this kind of visual conspicuousness because it is mostly active at night. Its daytime hours are spent resting in groups on mudflats or sandbars, where it can readily see predators and where the many watchful eyes of the flock make a surprise attack unlikely. When it does take flight, it utters a loud three-note *wee-a-whew*.

This bird ranges from the tropical forests of equatorial South America and Africa to the temperate marshes and shallow lakes of southern Africa and Argentina. It occupies habitats ranging from fresh to brackish waters, and from wilderness areas to sewage lagoons or farm ponds. Generally, open-country and freshwater habitats seem to be favored. It feeds by wading as well as swimming and diving, and consumes a variety of plant and invertebrate life.

Although pair bonds are strong in all whistling ducks, the White-faced is unique in that paired birds spend much time in mutual preening. Most of this preening is directed toward the white areas of the partner's head region, suggesting that this is an important social signal for stimulating preening activity. Otherwise, the birds have typical whistling duck displays, including a postcopulatory "step-dance," with both birds rising in the water and lifting the far wing vertically while calling. Breeding in both Africa and tropical South America is timed to coincide with the rainy season.

Nests are built on dry land or in shoreline reed beds, and 8 to 12 eggs are usually laid. Observations of wild birds in Venezuela indicate that incubation (by both parents) requires 30 or 31 days. Like giant bumblebees, the extremely attractive ducklings are a strongly patterned yellow and black. They require about 60 to 70 days to fledge. Predators, such as foxes, lizards, and Caracara hawks, often take the eggs, and storks (Jabiru and Maguairi) and caimans capture a considerable number of young.

These birds are very common over much of their broad range and do not appear to be threatened in any part of it.

🌐 Cuban Whistling Duck

(Dendrocygna arborea)

Adult Cuban Whistling Ducks

© Tom McHugh/Photo Researchers, Inc.

The Cuban, or West Indian, Whistling Duck has what is probably the smallest overall range of any of the whistling ducks, although paradoxically it is also the largest species. It occurs from the Bahamas south through Cuba, Hispaniola, and Puerto Rico to the northern Lesser Antilles (the Leeward Islands and Martinique).

This duck is strongly patterned with dark brown and white spots on its flanks, making it outwardly resemble the Spotted Whistling Duck. However, it has more in common structurally and behaviorally with the Black-bellied Whistling Duck. More arboreal than most of the whistling ducks, it not only regularly perches in trees but also often nests in them. Nests are often located in the branches of palms and among clumps of arboreal plants, and are sometimes situated quite high above ground. Few nests have been found in the wild, thus very little is known of the species' breeding biology. Like other whistling ducks, it is semi-nocturnal, and apparently feeds largely on the fruits of royal palms.

The clutch is reputed to average about nine eggs, and based on observations from captivity, the incubation period has been estimated at 30 days. The ducklings' plumage reveals this bird's evolutionary relationships inasmuch as its pattern more closely resembles that of the Black-bellied Whistling Duck than that of the Spotted Whistling Duck. This provides a good example of the generally more taxonomically instructive value of natal rather than adult plumages among waterfowl. Nothing is known of brood-rearing behavior in the wild, and the fledging period is also still unreported.

In Jamaica, Cuba, and Puerto Rico the Cuban Whistling Duck has suffered greatly from the introduction of the mongoose as well as hunting, and is perhaps locally threatened as a result. Although it has been given protected status in the Bahamas, Cuba, Jamaica, Puerto Rico, and the Virgin Islands, in some of these areas its numbers are still declining.

Black-bellied Whistling Duck

(Dendrocygna autumnalis)

Adult Black-bellied Whistling Duck

Like the White-faced Whistling Duck, this species breaks the "rules" of camouflage; its underparts are darker than its upper body. In any case, the striking black-and-white wing patterns exhibited by this bird in flight, its loud multi-syllable call, and its bright pink bill all conspire to make this one of the most attractive of the whistling ducks. It is widespread, ranging from the southern United States south through Mexico and Central America to northern Argentina. Tropical lagoons and swamps are favored habitats, as are rice paddies, but the bird rarely strays far from trees, which are frequently used for nesting.

The nesting period, at least in tropical areas, coincides with the wet season. Apparently this duck prefers cavity- rather than ground-nesting sites, particularly when the cavity is close to water. Like many cavity-nesting ducks, females are prone to lay their eggs in common sites, resulting in dump-nests that may at times hold large numbers of eggs, most of which never hatch. In Texas, the average clutch-size is about 13 eggs, with 18 observed in one study. Renesting after the loss of a complete clutch is probably fairly common. Incubation lasts about 28 to 31 days and is performed by both parents. Evidence suggests that pair-bonding may be permanent in this species.

This duck is common to abundant over most of its range.

White-backed Duck

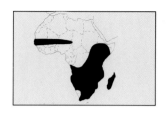

(*Thalassornis leuconotus*)

Adult White-backed Duck

The White-backed Duck is one of those rather mysterious and little-studied ducks that have long puzzled taxonomists, who typically like to place organisms in neat and tidy boxes. When it was discovered by T. C. Eyton in 1838, he thought this species might be a connecting link between the Musk Duck and the sea duck group. However, like more modern taxonomists, he failed to notice that, like whistling ducks, the White-backed Duck has a network-like tarsal pattern of scales on the lower leg, which is generally regarded as a primitive trait in waterfowl. This and a few other clues led me to suspect that the species had been misclassified as a stiff-tailed duck for years, and I finally was able to satisfy myself that it is in fact a somewhat aberrant whistling duck. Later studies confirmed this conclusion.

My first opportunities to study the breeding behavior of White-backed Ducks occurred in 1966, when a pair nested at the Wildfowl Trust in England. The nest was built near water in reeds and annual weeds close to a public pathway. This allowed me to closely observe the birds and to determine that both sexes help incubate, as in whistling ducks. When not incubating, the male stood close guard on the nest, fiercely threatening both humans and other bird species anytime it was approached. The eggs were unusually large (an adaptation for producing highly precocial chicks that can dive soon after hatching) and a pale rusty brown, rather than nearly white as in stifftails and whistling ducks.

They were incubated under broody hens, and hatched in 29 to 33 days. The ducklings of this species are patterned in a unique manner, but one that resembles the distinctive whistling duck pattern. The downy young were also found to have distress calls much like those of whistling ducks, and completely different from any species of stifftail.

White-backed Ducks are not very attractive birds, and only occasionally exhibit their white backs by wing-flapping or, even more rarely, taking flight. All their foraging is apparently done by diving, and they tend to remain submerged for fairly long periods of up to 30 seconds, even in shallow waters. Ducklings mostly or exclusively feed on gnat larvae obtained from muddy pond bottoms, but adults probably mainly eat the seeds of aquatic plants, as well as water lily leaves. They apparently do not forage at night as do typical whistling ducks. Pair bonds are seemingly very strong and perhaps permanent.

Although the African population is secure, nothing is known of the species' status in Madagascar.

Freckled Duck

(*Stictonetta naevosa*)

Male Freckled Duck

© B. Gadsby/VIREO

THE FRECKLED DUCK OF AUSTRALIA IS PRESENTED HERE AS THE SOLE representative of a unique tribe of ducks, although traditionally it has simply been considered an atypical or aberrant dabbling duck. From the time that I first read of the Freckled Duck, I wanted desperately to study its behavior. Finally, I was able to fund a trip to Australia in the 1960s.

Although I learned little about the species' social displays during this trip, it was enough to convince me that this indeed was a bird having many archaic waterfowl features, and that it should be separated from the dabbling ducks to emphasize this point. I was impressed by the similarity of the bill shape to that of *Oxyura* stifftails, and of the plumage and bill colors to those of Black-headed Ducks. Both led me to believe that perhaps the Freckled Duck provides an evolutionary link to this otherwise rather distinctive part of the family Anatidae. I proposed that the species be placed in a unique tribe within the subfamily Anserinae (in which whistling ducks, geese, and swans also are placed).

Since then, observations of captive birds have been made in Australia, and I was also able to watch two captive males and a female at the Wildfowl Trust. One display that has been described from these captive studies is the "axel-grind," performed only by males and usually directed toward females. The name of the display describes the strange grunting, almost squeaking, of the associated call, uttered as the male extends and turns his head from side to side while inclining his bill downward. No other waterfowl species has a display remotely like this, so it does not help directly in understanding the species' real relationships. However, some acoustic similarities exist between the axel-grind and the male display calls of the Black-headed Duck and Musk Duck, suggesting that a somewhat remote evolutionary connection between the Freckled Duck and the stifftails may exist.

Soon after mating the pair bond evidently breaks down, and the male plays no further direct role in breeding. However, males do defend a small area around a potential nest site. Clutches are usually of five to seven eggs, and incubation requires about 28 days. Females are highly defensive of their broods, which fledge at about nine weeks of age.

Because the Freckled Duck is a somewhat unwary bird, it is threatened by hunting as well as wetland drainage.

Shelducks

© D. Whitford/NHPA

Australian Shelduck female and young

The SHELDUCKS AND SHELDGEESE ARE A GROUP OF BIRDS THAT STRUC-
turally and behaviorally fall between the typical geese and swans
and the typical ducks, with features that help us to understand the evolutionary trends apparent in the entire family. Quite possibly the earli-
est species of waterfowl were a mixture of tropically distributed, large,
goose-like forms (similar to the present-day Magpie Goose of Australia)
and smaller duck-like birds (perhaps similar to the present-day Freckled Duck or the whistling ducks). From this central group, two broad
trends seem to have developed. One led to a group of generally large
species with strong pair bonds and bi-parental care of the nest and
young. These birds have long lifespans and fairly low reproductive
rates, as reflected in their small average clutch-sizes and delayed sexual
maturity. The other led to a group of smaller species having weaker,
annually renewed pair bonds, and higher reproductive rates, as indicated by their large average clutch-sizes and earlier sexual maturity.

The first group evolved or retained plumages that tend to camouflage them in the case of many of the smaller species, such as most

whistling ducks and geese. However, the largest and most highly territorial species, the northern swans, could afford to have conspicuous white plumages and trumpeting calls, because their size protected them from nearly all predators. The second group evolved plumages that tend to vary both between sexes and seasonally throughout the year. The latter is attained by molting more than once a year, rather than having a single annual molt. Thus, females typically evolved dully colored plumages, which are effective for hiding when incubating their eggs, whereas males evolved brighter, usually contrasting or even iridescent plumages, which are effective when competing for mates by either attracting females or dominating other males. For those times of the year when bright colors are not needed, a second molt produces a duller, female-like "eclipse" plumage, which provides effective camouflage.

Males in both groups also tended to evolve vocalizations that differ from those of females. In most species these include loud, often whistling, calls during courtship. The combination of special male plumages, calls, and elaborate courtship posturing provides a means of sexual and species identification by females during courtship, in addition to helping to identify those males having the greatest individual fitness for transmitting the species' genes.

The sheldgeese and shelducks are in a somewhat transitional state between these two groups. They typically have a prolonged period of sexual immaturity, lasting at least two and in some cases three years, and in most species clutch-sizes are fairly small. Many species (especially sheldgeese) show no seasonal variation in adult plumages, but in the majority the sexes differ noticeably in plumage coloration or body mass or both. The males are usually larger and considerably more aggressive than the females. Among shelducks, males are not necessarily more colorful than females; both sexes exhibit iridescent speculum patches, which are widespread in the true ducks and provide important social signaling devices through "ritualized" preening displays or other activities. Of equal importance is the females' inciting behavior toward favored males, which indicates that they have "chosen" such birds as potential mates. Males respond to inciting by either threatening potential rivals (the usual response in sheldgeese and shelducks) or by more strongly directing their courtship displays toward the inciting female. In this way a pair bond is gradually developed between the male and female, which might persist through the entire breeding season (as in shelducks and sheldgeese) or at least until the female has been fertilized and laid a clutch of eggs to be defended by her alone (as in the majority of true ducks). The length and strength of the pair bond is variable in true ducks, with males of temperate- and arctic-breeding species typically breaking the bond about the time the female begins incubation, and males of tropical-nesting ducks often remaining near the female to either help rear the young or refertilize her should a second nesting effort be necessary.

Scott Nielsen

Male and female New Zealand Shelducks

Ruddy Shelduck

(Tadorna ferruginea)

George K. Peck

*Female Ruddy Shelduck
(foreground)*

The Ruddy Shelduck ranges across much of central and southern Eurasia, extending from the Mediterranean shorelines east to central or eastern China and south in winter to India and Indochina. Its generally cinnamon brown color, with contrasting white upper wing coverts (feathers) and an iridescent green wing speculum, distinguish it readily from all other ducks of the region. It does, however, resemble the Cape Shelduck of Africa, which is certainly its nearest living relative, but lacks the gray head tones of that species. During the breeding season, the male has a narrow black collar that the female and immatures lack, whereas the female and young have whitish areas on the cheeks and forehead. The male tends to lose its black neck markings once the breeding season is over, suggesting that at least this part of the body plumage is molted twice a year. Young birds come to resemble adults during their first year, although initial breeding probably does not occur before their second year.

Before breeding, pair bonds are formed or re-formed by the combination of female inciting—a nattering call with associated bill-pointing movements—and the favored male's response, which is a loud, deeper hooting, with aggressive threats toward any opponent alternated with a haughty posturing toward the female. The male of a pair strongly defends the territory within which the female nests.

The nest is usually built in a natural cavity, such as a hollow tree, rock crevice, or abandoned ground burrow. Clutches average eight or nine eggs, which are incubated for 28 or 29 days by the female, while the male stands guard nearby. Both parents tend the young, which fledge in about 55 days and become independent shortly thereafter. Pair or family bonds evidently persist into winter, although it is uncertain whether pair bonds persist from year to year.

This bird is fairly common across much of its range.

Cape Shelduck

(Tadorna cana)

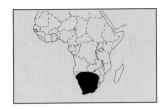

Male Cape Shelduck

Scott Nielsen

The Cape, or South African, Shelduck has the most restricted range of any shelduck; it is limited to South Africa and adjoining Namibia and Botswana. It is the only duck of that region having a mostly cinnamon- to chestnut-colored body, with white wing coverts and a green speculum (mainly visible in flight). The adult male has a uniformly gray head, whereas the female has a gray and white one. The plumage of the male is somewhat duller during the non-breeding season. In their first autumn of life juveniles are dull-colored birds, which closely resemble the young of Ferruginous Shelducks, with buff-gray heads and slightly lighter face markings. The adult vocalizations of the Cape and the Ruddy Shelducks are also very similar, with females having loud, nattering calls and males more goose-like honking or grunting notes.

Although adult plumages are attained within the first year of life, initial breeding probably occurs at two years of age. Pair bonds are believed to be fairly permanent, but are probably reinforced or renewed each year by territorial and courtship activities. Breeding occurs during the dry season, when the birds move to small areas of permanent fresh water, and establish or re-establish territories. These territories may or may not include within their boundaries potential nest sites, which are primarily abandoned burrows dug by aardvarks, spring hares, African porcupines, or other mammals.

Clutch-sizes are fairly large, averaging about ten eggs, and incubation by the female lasts some 30 days. After the young hatch, parents keep them mostly within the original territory, which may gradually expand as the young develop. They are kept well away from other shelduck families, probably to avoid hostile interactions. The young become independent and their families begin to break up at about ten weeks of age, when they learn to fly. Flocks develop that consist of nomadic groups of both unsuccessful breeders and unpaired birds, and very large flocks, which at times number tens of thousands, gather on the few large freshwater reservoirs and lakes that are favored molting areas. After completing their molts, the birds begin to move to shallow, brackish, and temporary pans for the remainder of the non-breeding period.

This species is quite common within its limited South African range.

Australian Shelduck

(Tadorna tadornoides)

Male Australian Shelduck

Jean-Paul Ferrero/Auscape

This species is often called the Mountain Duck in Australia, although it is essentially a lowland bird, usually found around the muddy shores of lakes, estuaries, and billabongs, or even along coastal shorelines. Adults can survive on salt water, but newly hatched chicks need fresh water for their first week or so. This duck is limited to the southern and western portions of Australia and is surprisingly absent from the well-watered areas along the eastern and northeastern coasts. It is readily distinguished from other Australian waterfowl by its chestnut-colored breast and conspicuous white wing coverts (often invisible in swimming or standing birds). Its diet consists of a diversity of plant and animal materials, especially green plants and aquatic insect life.

Initial breeding occurs in the second year of life. However, pair bonds may be changed frequently, especially among pairs that failed to produce young the previous season. Sexual displays of the male include mock-preening, chin-lifting, and head-shaking. The female primarily uses inciting as a means of stimulating male display behavior and selecting a specific male as a potential mate.

Like other shelducks, the Australian Shelduck is highly territorial. Territories established by the male may contain nest sites, or these may be several miles away. The brood-raising territories always contain fresh water, and may consist of about 50 to 200 yards (45 to 180 m) of shoreline and adjoining water, or a few acres of wetlands. Males accompany their mates to the nest site each day, but then return to defend the brooding territory. Eight to ten eggs are typically laid in a cavity nest, such as a tree hole or, where trees are lacking, a rabbit burrow. After hatching, the young are protected by both parents until they are able to fly at about 70 days. At this time, the families break up.

The Australian Shelduck is a common species over its range.

New Zealand Shelduck

(*Tadorna variegata*)

*Female New Zealand
Shelduck*

The counterpart to the Australian Shelduck in New Zealand, this species is commonly known in that country as the Paradise Shelduck. The two species are very similar, and certainly are very closely related; however, the New Zealand Shelduck generally has darker body plumage, especially on the breast. The female has an entirely white head, making it the most attractive of all the "typical" shelducks. Interestingly, the female exhibits a greater seasonal plumage change than does the male, shifting from a dark and rather male-like body plumage in the non-breeding season to a more rusty brown during breeding. Juveniles typically resemble adult males during their first autumn, but may have some white on the face and around the eyes in a pattern resembling that of the female Australian Shelduck. The adult plumage is attained during the first winter.

Initial breeding does not occur until the second year (in most males but only about half the females) or even the third. Once pair bonds are formed, the birds are monogamous and apparently have lifetime breeding associations. Breeding occurs only if the males are able to establish and hold territories; thus, some pairs may be unable to breed in their second year unless they have established a preliminary territory the year before. Established pairs re-form their bonds after the molting period and reclaim their territories. Should a mate have died in the interim, a new pair bond is quickly formed. The strong importance of territorial establishment and male dominance makes aggressive behavior (female inciting and inter-male threats or fighting) an important component of courtship. Males are initially chosen by the females but, if beaten in these contests, they are soon abandoned in favor of stronger males.

Like other shelducks, females of this species seek out tree holes, hollow logs, rabbit burrows, rock crevices, or other cavities for their nests. A clutch of eight to ten eggs is laid and incubated by the female for about 32 or 33 days, while the male guards the nearby territory. The male returns to the nest at the time of hatching, when the entire family moves to a nursery area within the breeding territory. Both sexes strongly defend their brood until they fledge at about eight weeks of age.

This species is common and widespread.

Northern Shelduck

(*Tadorna tadorna*)

Male Northern Shelduck

This is the "Common" Shelduck of Eurasia. In its case, the vernacular name shelduck is appropriate because, at least in adult males, it does have a definite shield-like enlargement at the base of the bill. This species differs from all other shelducks in one important regard—its diet is highly specialized and primarily consists of small mussels, especially an estuarine snail (*Hydrobia*). This snail is extremely common along coastal estuaries and saltmarsh flats, in sandy and muddy areas. The bird feeds by standing on shore in shallow water and probing with its sensitive bill for the snails. Although it at times upends in water of moderate depth, it never dives for food.

The Northern Shelduck is the most colorful of all the shelducks, with a conspicuous patterning of iridescent green (on the head), white (on the upper breast, flanks, back, and wings), and chestnut (on the lower breast). Like the other shelducks, it has iridescent green speculums and white upper wing coverts, which flash when it is in flight. Both sexes have bright red bills, and the male's is enlarged at the base. This strongly patterned adult appearance would suggest that the bird is probably highly territorial, and that bright coloration and conspicuous display behavior assure successful breeding.

Some females pair when only a year old, most pair and breed at two, and others may not breed until four or even five. Once established, pairs tend to persist from year to year, even during the winter flocking period. If a male dies during the breeding season, the female usually remains on their territory until she is joined by a new male; however, if the female dies, the male usually returns to the flock. Territories are maintained by a pair from year to year.

The nesting site may be miles away from the feeding territory, and often consists of an unused rabbit burrow. The seven to nine eggs are incubated by the female for 29 to 31 days. The young are quickly led from their nest to the foraging area, where they remain until the adults begin to leave for molting areas. Then the young gather in large groups or crèches, which are tended by non-breeders or failed breeders. Fledging occurs at 45 to 50 days, after which the young are fully independent.

This species is not in any danger at present.

Radjah Shelduck

(*Tadorna radjah*)

Male Radjah Shelduck

The Radjah Shelduck is a beautiful little white-headed shelduck with nearly white eyes and a blackish breastband that interrupts its otherwise white underparts. Like other shelducks, it has iridescent green speculums, but in this species they are bordered with a black bar in front and a white bar behind. The back color varies from brown (in Australia) to black (in the East Indian population), and the sexes are essentially identical in appearance, although the female has a slightly narrower black breastband than the male. Only their voices—a querulous rattling in females and a wheezy whistle in males—serve to identify the sexes easily.

These birds are strongly monogamous and probably retain permanent pair bonds after they mature, presumably at two years of age. They breed solitarily, and at the start of the season establish and defend a territory that includes a nest site (usually a hollow tree), a foraging area, and a brood-rearing area. This territory may include as much as 2 miles (3 km) of river frontage.

Little is known of the species' biology in nature, but the birds apparently forage mostly on mollusks and other aquatic invertebrates, and may remain on their breeding territories as pairs or family groups throughout the dry non-breeding season if water conditions permit. Pair-bonding consists of the usual shelduck pattern of female inciting and male responses of a sexual (toward the female) or aggressive (toward rival males) nature. Territorial disputes probably serve as a pair-bonding mechanism.

The normal clutch-size in nature is uncertain, as it seems to be frequently inflated by dumpnesting tendencies, but probably averages fewer than ten eggs. Incubation is believed to last about 30 days, and the young are tended by both parents; however, no specific information on this phase is available from observations of wild birds.

Populations of this duck in Australia and New Guinea are apparently declining, but no estimates are available.

Steamer Ducks

Female Flightless Steamer Ducks

© Robert W. Hernandez/Photo Researchers, Inc.

THE SOUTH AMERICAN STEAMER DUCKS ARE AN UNUSUAL GROUP OF LARGE diving ducks. In some ecological ways they are very similar to Northern Hemisphere eiders, but they have clearly evolved from shelduck-like ancestors, and indeed they are most often simply grouped with the shelducks. However, several recent studies have suggested that they should probably be given separate tribal recognition. A study by Bradley Livezey of the University of Kansas indicates that, although they derive from the shelducks, they show some surprising anatomical similarities to the South American Torrent Duck and the Blue Duck of New Guinea. Such similarities are quite possibly the result of the evolution of comparable traits related to diving. In addition, the species boundaries of the steamer ducks are uncertain at present, with the several flightless forms of steamer ducks showing a degree of variation in plumage and size somewhat comparable to that of the Common Eider. Additionally steamer ducks have been little studied in the wild. Thus, in this book all flightless steamer ducks will be collectively considered as a single generalized type.

Flying Steamer Duck

(Tachyeres patachonicus)

Male Flying Steamer Duck

This is the smallest of the steamer ducks, although adults weigh about 5 pounds (2 kg), which is more than any of the Northern Hemisphere ducks except the eiders. It also has the longest wings of any steamer duck. Unless a headwind is available, however, it must "steam" along for some distance before becoming airborne.

It nests on freshwater ponds, lakes, and rivers near the coast, or occasionally as far as 30 miles (50 km) from the beach, gradu- ally moving to coastal waters during the fall and winter, when some flocking occurs, especially among molting and non-breeding birds. Crabs, other crustaceans, and thick-shelled mollusks are its main food. It finds these along the bottoms of tidal waters near shore and swallows them whole or perhaps, in the case of crabs, first crushes and kills them with its heavy bill. Like true diving ducks, the steamer duck has feet with strongly lobed hind toes. These help propel it during its underwater foraging.

The Flying Steamer Duck is more freshwater-oriented and generally more brownish-colored than the flightless steamer ducks, which it probably competes with for food to a limited degree where their habitats overlap. Little is known of its courtship displays, but presumably interspecies dif- ferences do exist, which help to avoid hybridization. What is known is that male displays seem to be related to territorial estab- lishment and defense, and include overt fighting. Female displays are rather similar to those of males, and are not yet known to include inciting behavior, although a "stretching" display of the female may serve this role.

All steamer ducks nest on the ground, typically on small islets surrounded by water, and they have fairly small clutches of about seven eggs. The male remains near the nest to help protect the female, and later remains with her while the young are being reared. Detailed information on the incu- bation and brood-rearing phases of all steamer ducks is still lacking. It is likely that at least two years are required before adulthood is attained.

Although no population figures are available, this species is seem- ingly common over its range.

Flightless Steamer Ducks

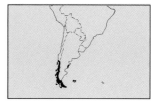

(*Tachyeres* spp.)

Female Flightless Steamer Duck

Several apparent species of flightless steamer ducks have been described by biologists, all of which are extremely similar in appearance and can readily be dealt with collectively here. In southern Chile and Tierra del Fuego, the Magellanic Flightless Steamer Duck (*T. pteneres*) occurs. It is replaced to the east on the Falkland Islands by the Falkland Flightless Steamer Duck (*T. brachypterus*) and farther north in Chubut, Argentina, by a population recently described as a new species, the White-headed Flightless Steamer Duck (*T. leucocephala*). It seems likely that the Flying Steamer Duck is the ancestral type of steamer duck and has given rise to these similar but even larger and essentially flightless forms in these areas. Perhaps these enormous ducks—some old males weigh up to 10 pounds (4.5 kg)—are better able to dive and exploit the rich mussels that grow in these cold subantarctic waters. Differences in the sizes of the adult sexes may also allow males to dive deeper and feed on larger prey than can females.

In the case of the Falkland Flightless Steamer Duck, male territories are spaced at intervals of about 300 yards (275 m). These territories include both the offshore foraging areas and the shoreline back to the vegetation's edge. Nests are placed in grass tussocks, other vegetation such as dried kelp, or even in old penguin burrows, at times as far as a quarter mile (0.5 km) away from the beach. The male guards the beachfront during the month-long incubation period, and alerts the female to any sign of danger. Both parents care for the young, with the larger male often assuming the role of primary defender, while the female leads their brood to safety. It probably requires about four months to bring the young to independence, although they never fledge in the sense of acquiring the ability to fly.

No population figures are available, but the White-headed Flightless Steamer Duck is believed to be rare.

© R. Van Nostrand/ Photo Researchers, Inc.

Perching Ducks

Peter Cook/Auscape

Female Green Pygmy Goose

THE PERCHING DUCKS ARE A STRANGE GROUP OF BIRDS THAT SEEM TO range from primitive-appearing, somewhat goose-like birds, such as the Comb Duck and Muscovy Duck, to small, elegant, and highly attractive species, such as the Ringed Teal, Brazilian Teal, American Wood Duck, and Mandarin Duck. Indeed, in a recently published taxonomy of the family by Bradley Livezey, the group was split into several groups, with the Spur-winged Goose and the Comb Duck grouped with the shelducks rather than with the other species traditionally considered perching ducks. Of these more typical perching ducks, the pygmy geese, Australian Wood Duck, Ringed Teal, and Brazilian Teal were separated from the remainder, and were believed to be more closely related to the typical dabbling ducks. As a result, the "perching ducks" are probably an artificial assemblage. They are difficult if not impossible to characterize easily, but all of them except the large land-nesting Spur-winged Goose are hole-nesters. Consequently, they tend to be capable perching birds, with sharp claws and long, broad tails that probably help them land and remain perched on elevated tree branches. Females are often considerably smaller than males, a trait that has been attributed by some researchers to sexual selection and by others to the ability of small females to more readily find and use small tree cavities.

It is debatable whether the Spur-winged Goose should be considered a duck at all, because it certainly has few if any duck-like traits. Since Jean Delacour and Ernst Mayr revised the family's taxonomy in 1945, the Spur-winged Goose has been generally regarded as a member of the perching duck tribe. However, its skeletal anatomy, the composition of its eggshell, and the results of various studies all favor the view that it is either a species that falls between the perching ducks and the shelducks, or an aberrant shelduck. Because of its goose-like traits and uncertain taxonomic position, it will not be further discussed in this book.

Muscovy Duck

(Cairina moschata)

Female and male Muscovy Ducks

This bird and the Mallard are the only ducks that have ever been fully domesticated. For this reason, the Muscovy has acquired a worldwide distribution, at least in tropical and semi-tropical climates. Although the bird had already been domesticated by native peoples at the time of the Spanish conquest of South America during the sixteenth century, domesticated Muscovies never exhibit the degree of plumage and structural variation that has been attained in domestic Mallards. Domesticated Muscovies often show some of the iridescent purplish black plumage typical of wild birds, and males usually exhibit even larger areas of facial swelling (caruncles) than do the wild birds. The Muscovy's native home is the American tropics, from Mexico south through-out the warmer and more heavily wooded habitats of Central and South America. There it feeds on an extremely wide array of plants and other foods, including such unlikely prey as termites, other insects, or whatever else happens to be locally available.

In the wild, this bird typically nests in hollow trees, but it will also nest among the crowns of palms. Domesticated Muscovies often nest on the ground, among rushes or other vegetation. Like most cavity-nesting ducks, their clutch-sizes tend to be fairly large (it is much easier to incubate a large clutch in a confined area than on a flat surface). They average 10 to 12 eggs, but dump-nesting at times results in abnormally high numbers. Incubation lasts a rather long time, about 35 days, and is completed by the female alone. Indeed, it is unlikely that even wild Muscovies establish any pair bonds; males seem to associate with females only long enough to fertilize them. Females remain with their broods until fledging, but it is unlikely that family bonds persist much beyond that point.

The Muscovy is still locally common. No population estimates are available.

Paul Johnsgard

59

White-winged Wood Duck

(Cairina scutulata)

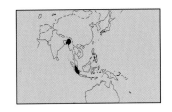

Male White-winged Wood Duck

reserve in Viet Nam, the most recent estimates for mainland Asia are of about 200 surviving individuals. There is no definite geographic variation throughout this range, although a good deal of individual variation in head and upper breast color occurs, perhaps as a result of local inbreeding. In most birds the head is heavily speckled with black in both sexes, but males generally have whiter heads, and in some cases not only the head but also the upper breast may be entirely white. In all birds the anterior upper wing coverts and underwing coverts are white, and the secondaries have a uniformly gray speculum that is bordered at the front with black.

Like the Muscovy Duck, the White-winged Wood Duck lives along tropical wooded streams or swamps, feeds on a wide diversity of plant and animal materials, and usually nests in hollow trees or perhaps other elevated sites, and apparently infrequently on the ground. In contrast to the Muscovy, pair bonds do appear to be present, and the male may remain to help rear and protect the brood.

This is one of the endangered species of ducks. Its original range probably included much of tropical southeastern Asia from Assam, India, east through nearly all of Indochina, as well as Sumatra and Java. In recent years it has been greatly reduced in numbers and range, and now is apparently confined to extreme northeastern India (Arunachal Pradesh and Manipur), Bangladesh, and southern Sumatra, with perhaps some also surviving in northern Myanmar, and possibly a few in Malaysia and Java. Recently found in Nam Cat Tien forest

© Joe Blossom/NHPA

*Male Comb Duck
(South American race)*

Comb Duck

(Sarkidiornis melanotos)

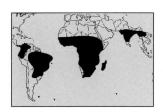

The Comb Duck, sometimes called the Knob-billed Goose, is an exotic-looking duck of South America and the Old World, where it ranges from tropical Africa to India and southeast Asia. In South America and southeastern Asia, it occurs in many of the same areas as do the Muscovy Duck and the White-winged Wood Duck. Unlike these species, it has whitish underparts. In the South American population the flanks are dark gray (females and immatures) to black (males), but in the Old World birds the flanks are a lighter gray in both sexes. The adult male, which is much larger than the female, has a distinctive black knob of fatty material growing up from the top of the bill. It probably is an indicator of the general vigor of the male, allowing females to "choose" a desirable mate.

Males have never been observed helping care for broods, indicating that pair bonds are probably very weak at best.

Nests may be placed in tall grassy cover, in tree hollows or crotches, and in abandoned tree nests of other birds. Clutches number 8 to 12 eggs, and incubation lasts about 30 days.

No population estimates are available. The Old World form is more widespread and seemingly more abundant than the New World one, which was judged threatened by Janet Kear and Gwyn Williams.

Female Hartlaub's Duck

Hartlaub's Duck

(Pteronetta hartlaubi)

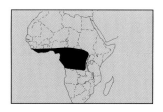

Although the Hartlaub's Duck has at times been included in genus *Cairina* with the Muscovy Duck and the White-winged Wood Duck, it is a smaller and more agile species than these. Like them, however, it is associated with tropical forests. Roughly Mallard-sized, it more closely approximates dabbling ducks in shape and posture than it does the larger perching ducks. The upper wing coverts of both sexes are distinctly bluish and the secondaries are a dark brown. The adult male has a varying amount of white on the head, ranging from a small patch on the cheeks to a completely white upper head.

This duck has been little studied, because of its inaccessible rainforest and wooded savanna habitats. It perches well and may nest in hollow trees, although no nests of wild birds have yet been described. Among captive birds, females have laid clutches of eight or nine eggs, which required an incubation period of 32 days.

No population estimates are available; however, this duck is dependent on tropical rainforests, which are declining.

Green Pygmy Goose

(*Nettapus pulchellus*)

Male and female Green Pygmy Geese

The three species of "pygmy geese" are misnamed—they are really pygmy perching ducks that have evolved short, rather goose-like bills for stripping grass seeds and clipping the flower heads and seeds of water lilies. They eat virtually no animal materials. Among the smallest of all waterfowl, they range in weight from about 8 to 15 ounces (230 to 420 g), and are among the most strikingly beautiful of all ducks, with strongly iridescent upper wing coverts. Two of the three species have contrasting white speculums that cover most of the secondary feathers, producing a pattern of brilliant flashing wings in flight. All pygmy geese take flight easily, and often call while flying, uttering high-pitched, often trilled or whistling calls that further help to identify them.

The Green Pygmy Goose of northern Australia and southern New Guinea has a beautifully penciled pattern of gray and white on the flanks and breast, and a generally two-toned head, with the upper half mostly brownish black and the cheeks mottled with black and white (in adults) or lightly penciled with gray (in young birds). The green of the upper wings extends to the back and, in the male, the sides of the neck, at least during breeding. During the non-breeding season, the male is slightly less iridescent on the head and neck.

Breeding occurs during the wet season, after the lagoons have filled to maximum size and the water lilies and other aquatic plants on which the bird depends have begun to grow luxuriantly. Pairing may be permanent, but little is known of the species' pair-maintaining or pair-forming displays. The male does seek out possible nesting sites and point them out to the female, which then selects one.

The nest sites are always in tree hollows, but may also be placed among swamp vegetation or on fairly dry ground. Little is known of clutch-size (probably 8 to 12 eggs), and the incubation period is unreported.

This species is common locally in northern Australia and generally abundant in New Guinea.

Cotton Pygmy Goose

(Nettapus coromandelianus)

George K. Peck

Male Cotton Pygmy Goose

This is the smallest and most widespread of the pygmy geese, ranging from western India east to southern China, Taiwan, the Philippines, and at least locally extending over much of the East Indies as far as New Guinea and northeastern Australia. Although often also called the Cotton Teal, it has nothing to do with cotton. Instead, the name refers to the mostly white appearance of the male, especially during the breed-ing season, when it has a mostly white head, breast, and flanks, attractively punctuated with a black crown, breastband, back, and tail. In flight, the male utters a rapid series of cackling notes sounding like a repeated *fix bayonets, fix bayonets,* and the female reportedly utters softer quacking notes. The adult bird is highly aquatic, feeding mainly on pond-weeds and the seeds of various aquatic and shoreline grasses.

The Cotton Pygmy Goose breeds during the wet season, when the swamps are at their maximum levels and aquatic foods are easily available. Little is known of its courtship behav-ior, but because the male has quite different breeding and non-breeding eclipse plumages, it seems likely that pair bonds are established every year rather than permanently retained.

Nests are placed in elevated sites, most often hollow trees, although other sites are some-times used, such as chimneys or even holes in the walls of tem-ples or houses. Clutch-sizes seem to average about eight to ten, but nests (possibly dump-nests) con-taining up to 16 eggs have been found. The incubation period is uncertain, and the role of the male in brood care is not yet clear. It would seem that both sexes of these tiny ducks would be needed to care for such tiny and highly vulnerable ducklings.

Although abundant in India, this bird is less common in southeastern Asia. The Aus-tralian population is very small, probably numbering in the low thousands.

63

African Pygmy Goose

(Nettapus auritus)

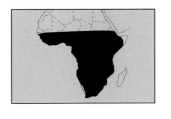

Male African Pygmy Goose

Some people might argue that this is the most beautiful of all ducks. Unlike the Mandarin and North American Wood Duck, the male does not lose his glorious coloration when the breeding season is over. Both sexes have a stunning white speculum set off against otherwise dark green to blackish wings, chestnut flanks and breasts, and a whitish underpart and face pattern. The male differs from the female in having a black-edged area of iridescent green on the rear of the head and upper neck, a sharply defined black crown, and a bright yellow, black-tipped bill. Often found perching on a low, partly submerged tree, this bird adds a touch of brilliant color to a tropical forest pond scene. Like other pygmy geese, it is a dainty bird, floating as lightly on the water as a brightly colored autumn leaf, and occasionally plucking seeds from a water lily, or even diving for food.

It is usually found in small flocks, perhaps representing family groups, and pair bonds may be fairly permanent, inasmuch as no seasonal plumage variation exists, breeding seasons are seemingly variable, and the birds do not appear to migrate (pair bonds are often broken in migrating birds). Pair bonds of captive birds seem to be strong, even outside the breeding season.

Nesting probably occurs during the warmer and wetter parts of the year. Nests are typically in tree hollows as high as 80 feet (25 m) above ground, but have also been found in cliff holes, termite nests, and even in a cavity in the roof thatching of a hut. Surface-nesting in thick grass clumps has also been reported, so the birds may be quite flexible in this regard. In common with Green Pygmy Geese, the male is said to accompany the female when the pair is nest-hunting. The typical clutch-size in captive birds numbers about nine eggs, with a maximum of 12. African Pygmy Geese have bred only rarely in captivity, but in one case incubation was found to require 23 or 24 days, which is a very short time for a cavity-nesting duck. The role of the male in helping care for the brood is uncertain.

Although widespread, this species is very local in its distribution. No population estimates are available.

Ringed Teal

(*Callonetta leucophrys*)

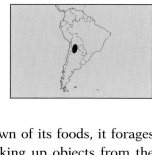

Male Ringed Teal

One of the most attractive of the teal-like ducks is this species, which occasionally has been grouped with the more typical teal in the genus *Anas*. However, in the 1960s I determined that the species' behavior has much more in common with the American Wood Duck, Mandarin, and especially Brazilian Teal, and re-classified it as a perching duck.

More recent anatomical studies have generally confirmed that conclusion.

In the wild state, the Ringed Teal has been poorly studied. It occurs from southern Brazil south to Argentina, where it inhabits mostly forested areas, especially marshes surrounded by forests, and periodically flooded lowlands. Although little is known of its foods, it forages by picking up objects from the water surface or just below it, and probably eats a variety of small seeds and perhaps some small invertebrates. The birds fly swiftly, with both sexes showing beautiful white wing patches on the upper wing coverts, in front of iridescent green speculums on their secondaries. Like female Mandarins and American Wood Ducks, the female Ringed Teal lacks quacking calls, but utters a sharp, cat-like note. Similarly, the male produces only a soft, wheezy whistle during courtship. Observed in captivity, the male's displays are quite simple postures and preening movements.

Ringed Teal have strong, possibly permanent pair bonds. Like most perching ducks, the female is a hole-nester, and in the wild often nests in the large stick nests of Monk Parakeets. Clutch-sizes number 6 to 12 eggs. Incubation, which lasts 26 to 28 days, is probably by the female alone, although males will at times enter the nesting hole to join the female. After hatching occurs, the male leads the family and plays a primary role in the defense and care of the brood.

No information is available on this species' numerical status, but it appears to be common locally.

American Wood Duck

(*Aix sponsa*)

Male and female American Wood Ducks

This duck is largely limited to wooded areas in North America, where it is most abundant east of the Great Plains and south of Canada. It has extended its range in recent decades, partly because of extensive nest box erection programs in areas where natural tree cavities are rare or lacking. Pair-bonding, which occurs in wintering areas, is marked by intense competition among the males. Once pair bonds have been formed, they seem quite strong, and the male takes an active role in seeking out suitable nest sites.

Tree cavities are typically used for nesting, although nest boxes are often chosen as well, especially if the female was hatched in one. Clutch-sizes often number 13 to 15 eggs, and incubation requires about 30 days. The male typically abandons its mate shortly before hatching, and the female rears the young alone for the 60-day fledging period.

Although Wood Duck populations were very low during the drought years of the 1930s, they have fully recovered.

Many people would vote for this species as the world's most beautiful duck. The male in breeding plumage has bright red eyes and is the only highly crested duck with white throat patches that curve up into the cheeks. The female and eclipse-plumage male are much less distinctly crested, and although the latter retains its red eyes and bill coloration, the female is very difficult to distinguish from the female Mandarin.

Scott Nielsen

66

❷ Mandarin

(*Aix galericulata*)

Male Mandarin

It is hard to imagine a more appropriate name for this species; its image served as one of the badges of rank among the mandarins. The Chinese and Japanese have held this duck in special esteem for thousands of years, and have used it as a wonderful symbol of happiness and marital fidelity. Appropriately, it is limited to the heart of the Orient in eastern China and Japan. Interestingly, a feral flock has recently become established in Great Britain and parts of northern Europe through the activities of aviculturists.

The male in full plumage has a pair of remarkable "sail" feathers that are vertically raised above the back, beautiful narrow chestnut feathers that hang down from the cheeks, and a broad white eye-stripe that is bounded above and below by darker feathers and terminates in a long, shaggy crest. The female is demurely patterned in gray and olive tones, but like the male has bluish iridescent speculums on its secondaries, which are bounded along the rear edge with narrow black and white stripes. The male in eclipse plumage resembles the female but has a reddish bill.

Like American Wood Ducks, Mandarins have beautiful courtship displays, which include shaking and mock-drinking. Pair bonds often persist between breeding seasons, and males accompany their mates on nest-site searches among the trees. Their incubation and brood-rearing biology is almost identical to that of American Wood Ducks.

Mandarins have declined greatly in both China and Japan, where they were once abundant. The entire Asian population may be under 20,000 birds. A few thousand also occur in England and Europe.

Australian Wood Duck

(*Chenonetta jubata*)

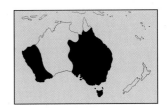

Female Australian Wood Duck

Australian Wood Ducks have strong pair bonds that, in the wild, often last more than a year and probably persist until one of the pair dies. No definite fixed breeding territory is established, although a "moving territory" around the female is defended by the male against sexual incursions by other males. Like American Wood Ducks, these birds mature in their first year and have an active period of competitive social display, during which females "select" their mates from among the competing males.

Nests are always located in tree cavities, and both members of the pair participate in searches for suitable sites. Clutch-sizes average 10 or 11 eggs, but these numbers might be inflated by dump-nesting tendencies. Incubation is said to range from 28 to 34 days. The young, which are closely attended by both parents through their entire 57-day fledging period, remain with their parents for a few weeks after gaining their flight abilities.

This species is common in much of its range with a population that probably numbers in the tens of thousands.

The scientific name of this species means "maned goose-duck," and indeed it has often been called the Maned Goose. Like the pygmy geese, it has a short, stout bill, which enables it to eat a variety of plant materials, ranging from seeds to, especially, leafy materials. In contrast to most perching ducks, this species lacks iridescent plumage altogether. Each wing does, however, have an immaculate white speculum on the secondaries, which is separated from the gray upper wing coverts by a narrow black boundary. The male has unusual black underparts, black hindquarters, and a small black "mane" on the hindneck. The female shows a somewhat stronger resemblance to female pygmy geese than to females of American Wood Ducks or Mandarin Ducks but, in common with them, has somewhat similar single-syllable self-identification calls. The male also utters distinctive, single-syllable, cat-like identity notes.

Brazilian Teal

(*Amazonetta brasiliensis*)

Brazilian Teal female and male with ducklings

This "teal" is another species that in the past has been grouped with typical teal in the genus *Anas* but that now appears to have somewhat closer affinities with the perching ducks, especially the Ringed Teal. Bradley Livezey of the University of Kansas recently concluded that these two ducks comprise the "sister-group" to the other *Anas*-like ducks, falling taxonomically between them and the typical perching ducks. Both sexes of Brazilian Teal have beautiful wing patterns, which are a stunning sight when the birds are in flight. A large iridescent green wing speculum, spreading to the inner primaries and larger wing coverts, is bounded along the rear first by a narrow black band and then by a white border. Both sexes also have sealing-wax red feet and legs, and the male's bill is similarly colored. The male utters a rather wheezy but loud and piercing whistle, whereas the female utters *Anas*-like quacking notes.

The Brazilian Teal occurs widely over the lowlands of South America east of the Andes, and in Venezuela it is widespread in wooded wetlands. In Venezuela it is non-migratory, and nests during the wet season. Although few nests have been found in the wild, the bird apparently can nest either in trees (on top of other birds' old nests) or on the ground in tunnel-like openings in sedges. The pair bond is strong, and perhaps permanent, and remating takes place rapidly after the loss of a mate. Clutches average six to eight eggs, and the incubation period is 25 to 29 days. The young, which are apparently tended by both parents during the fledging period, are able to fly in 60 to 70 days.

No population estimates are available, but this bird is apparently common in some parts of its range.

❧Torrent Duck
(*Merganetta armata*)

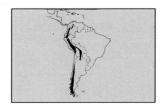

Male Torrent Duck
(Chilean race)

THE TORRENT DUCK IS THE SOLE SPECIES OF ITS GROUP. ONE OF THE MOST highly specialized of all species of ducks, it lives only in torrential streams flowing out of the snow-capped peaks of the South American Andes. It is a highly streamlined, slim-bodied, and long-tailed duck. Both sexes have bright red bills, green wing speculums bounded in front and behind with narrow white borders, and back feathers that are pointed and strongly striped with black and white. The bird's long tail feathers are much like those of stiff-tailed ducks and are used for propping itself on slippery rocks. Its bill, which is rather soft-edged and narrow, is used for probing for insects. This duck rarely flies far; instead, it dives or "rides" downstream when frightened. It also feeds by diving.

The Torrent Duck is similar in some ways to the torrent-dwelling Blue Duck of New Zealand; however, any similarities may be the result of chance evolutionary convergence. Probably the Torrent Duck evolved from a perching duck ancestor, although its displays are unique in many ways, and most people now agree that it deserves placement in a tribe of its own.

The birds seem to have strong, perhaps permanent pair bonds. Judging from the few nests so far found, they nest in diverse sites, such as kingfisher burrows, on steep cliffs, or at the base of bushes near streams. An extremely small clutch of only three or four eggs, laid at intervals of several days, seems typical. The incubation period has been estimated at 43 or 44 days, making it easily the longest of any known species of waterfowl, including the swans. The male joins the female periodically during the incubation period, and when the chicks have hatched the brood is quickly taken to water. The fledging period is unknown, but probably is rather prolonged because of the bird's specialized food needs. Being swept downstream by the swift currents is a major cause of chick mortality.

No detailed population estimates are available, but population densities are very low even in the pristine river habitats of the Andes, and the species may be endangered.

Dabbling Ducks

Darwin R. Wiggett/First Light

Female Green-winged Teal and duckling

THIS IS BY FAR THE LARGEST GROUP OF THE DUCKS, AND INCLUDES THE largest number of broadly distributed and more abundant species. Such successful birds as the Mallard and its close relatives occur almost throughout the world, and have probably achieved their success by being able to forage and breed in a wide variety of environments, from tropical to arctic. Many are also highly migratory, allowing them to use extreme environments (the arctic tundra, for example) only when weather conditions allow. Short incubation and fledging periods are common, and in extreme environments may allow them to reproduce in less than three months from the time they arrive.

Dabbling ducks range in size from small ("teal") species well under a pound (0.5 kg) in adult weight to some exceeding 3 pounds (1 kg). All are able to take flight from the water in a "leaping" (rather than running) manner, and are generally swift and elusive fliers that can escape most aerial predators. Most species nest on the ground, and in many the male plays no role in rearing the young. Yet, in several of the more tropically oriented species, pair bonds are strong and males regularly participate in brood care. These species often lack eclipse male plumages and remain bright-colored the year-around.

Pink-eared Duck

(Malacorhynchus membranaceous)

Male Pink-eared Duck

Traditionally, the Pink-eared Duck of Australia has been regarded as an atypical or aberrant dabbling duck, with superficial similarities to shovelers (it also feeds on planktonic organisms), but with no certain near relatives. In recent years, studies of its behavior and anatomy have led some researchers to believe that it should be included with the perching ducks, while others have suggested that it might have been derived from shelduck-like ancestral stock. Although this latter possibility seems unlikely, given the gentle nature of these birds, Bradley

Livezey's studies at the University of Kansas suggest that the Pink-eared Duck may be part of the same evolutionary branch or "clade" that produced the typical shelducks. Indeed, he considers it a highly derived shelduck. Because of its uncertain taxonomic position, it is here listed as the first of the dabbling ducks, in keeping with tradition.

The most remarkable feature of this duck is not its pink "ears" (small patches of pinkish feathers that are usually not visible) but rather its long shoveler-like bill, with soft pendant flaps at each side near the tip. The bill

has many closely spaced and comb-like extensions that strain extremely small food particles from the water, in a manner something like that of the flamingo. The Pink-eared Duck spends much of its time swimming about with its bill partly immersed, sometimes following directly behind another duck and gaining access to the foods stirred up by the other's paddling feet.

Pink-ears are very quiet, non-demonstrative ducks, and pair bonds are evidently fairly strong, possibly even lifelong. The birds can breed at any time of the year, depending upon when water levels are suitable for nesting. During the breeding season, the male defends an area around his mate and their nest or brood, but not a defined geographic territory.

The nest is usually located above water, on a tree crotch, in a tree hollow, stump, or the like, but also may be built in swamp grasses. About seven eggs are laid, and incubation by the female lasts about 26 days. After the young have hatched, they are cared for by both parents for an unknown period.

No population estimates are available for this duck. Local population counts fluctuate because it is a highly nomadic species; however, it is common over its range.

© Tom McHugh/Photo Researchers

Male and female Blue Duck
with duckling

The Blue Duck of New Zealand, like the Torrent Duck, is a highly specialized species limited to fast-flowing streams of both North and South islands. It is highly territorial, with each pair often spaced more than a half-

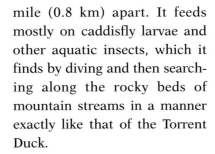

◐ Blue Duck

(*Hymenolaimus malacorhynchos*)

mile (0.8 km) apart. It feeds mostly on caddisfly larvae and other aquatic insects, which it finds by diving and then searching along the rocky beds of mountain streams in a manner exactly like that of the Torrent Duck.

Sexual maturity is reached and pair-bonding starts during the first year, but unless the males can attain and hold territories successfully, breeding will not occur. Once mated, pair bonds are held permanently.

The nest is placed within the

pair's territory, in such diverse sites as rock clefts, hollow logs, tree trunks, and clumps of grass. Clutch-sizes average only five or six eggs. The incubation period is 31 or 32 days, with the male remaining on territory close to the incubating female. The fledging period is about 70 days.

In 1990, the Blue Duck population was estimated at 2,000 to 4,000 birds and is probably declining.

Male Salvadori's Duck

The Salvadori's Duck of New Guinea is the third (the Andean Torrent Duck and New Zealand Blue Duck being the others) of the three species of ducks that have become highly specialized

Salvadori's Duck

(*Anas waigiuensis*)

for life in fast streams. However, this duck also lives on alpine lakes, so it is perhaps the least modified of the three. The sexes are similar in appearance. Males produce sharp whistled notes, whereas females utter dabbling-duck quacking sounds. Aquatic insects and larvae are known to be eaten, but detailed information on foods and foraging is limited.

The birds probably pair permanently, and seem to establish residential territories along stretches

of river. The few nests that have been found have been in depressions near water, usually under grass clumps or shrubs, rather than in tree hollows or other cavity sites. Clutches number three or four eggs, and the incubation period is probably also fairly long, although it is still undetermined. The male is known to accompany the female and young during the brood-rearing period, which exceeds two months.

This bird is locally common.

African Black Duck

(*Anas sparsa*)

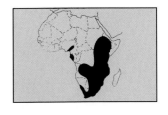

Male African Black Duck

P.J. Ginn

Like the Salvadori's Duck of New Guinea, this somewhat similar-appearing species is a river-adapted bird, but one that is less specialized for fast-water environments. Instead of being streamlined, it is a chunky, Mallard-like bird, which at least in some respects seems primitive rather than highly specialized. Besides living on fairly fast-flowing waters, the bird inhabits stagnant ponds and slow-moving waters, often in open and dry-country habitats. The bird can certainly dive when necessary, and has been seen negotiating small waterfalls and steep rapids; however, it evidently consumes a wide array of foods and is not dependent upon those from fast-water environments.

Both sexes resemble American Black Ducks but have a darker black plumage and sharply contrasting white or buff barring and spotting on the back. They have Mallard-like blue speculum patterns on their wings, bounded in front and behind with black and white borders. The female often quacks loudly but seems to lack the decrescendo calls typical of most *Anas* females. When the female incites, the male's response often consists of head-pumping. The male also seems to lack some of the typical Mallard-like courtship displays (such as the down-up) or exhibits them in only a rudimentary manner (head-up-tail-up).

Pair bonds are probably maintained indefinitely. A permanent home range is maintained and defended throughout the year by paired birds. Only holders of territory attempt to breed.

The nest is usually placed on the ground, although some cavity sites have been found. It is typically hidden among grassy or other cover such as flood debris, close to water, and a fairly small clutch of four to eight eggs is laid. The incubation period is 28 days. When the young hatch, they are accompanied only by the female, although the male may join them for nocturnal roosting. About 80 to 90 days are required before the young acquire a fully developed plumage.

Population estimates are not available for this species. It is widespread, but only locally common.

Eurasian Wigeon

(Anas penelope)

Male Eurasian Wigeon

Thomas Kitchin

The Eurasian, or "Common," Wigeon, is widespread throughout northern Eurasia. It has become increasingly common in North America in recent decades; scattered birds turn up with regularity every year and have now been reported from virtually every state and province. However, nesting in North America still remains undocumented. Like all wigeons, both sexes have white upper wing coverts (mottled with gray in the female) and green speculums. The male has a distinctive cinnamon red head and neck, with a buff crown and forehead. The female (and young as well as eclipse-plumaged males) closely resembles the female of the American Wigeon, but has a somewhat darker brown head, as well as a generally darker brown (less rufous-tinted) breast and flanks. No doubt it is the similarity of the females of these two species that has thus far prevented the documentation of Eurasian Wigeons nesting in North America.

Like all wigeons, the male utters rather loud, whistling notes during courtship and when alarmed, and indeed seems to lack low-pitched notes altogether. Also in common with other wigeons, the bird is an adept grazer, using its short bill for clipping grasses in a goose-like manner. It engages in prolonged social courtship during the winter and spring, when the loud whistling notes of the males become highly evident, and the displaying birds raise the tips of their folded wings above the back so far that their iridescent secondaries become visible.

The female prefers nesting in cover that has shrubs, and the nest is usually extremely well hidden under such vegetation. The clutch averages about nine eggs, and incubation by the female lasts about 24 days. No help is provided by the male, which by hatching time has often begun to molt, sometimes at considerable distances from the nesting area.

This species is abundant, probably numbering a million or more birds.

American Wigeon

(Anas americana)

Male American Wigeon

Like the "Bald" Eagle, the American Wigeon has traditionally been called the Baldpate by many Americans, in reference to the white feathered area on the crown or "pate" of the male when in breeding plumage. American Wigeon is certainly preferable, as it is a close relative of the Eurasian Wigeon and Chiloe Wigeon. (The origin of "wigeon" is somewhat uncertain, but it may imitate the male's whistling call.) As noted in the previous account, an expert eye is needed to distinguish females of the American and Eurasian Wigeon. Rather than being distinctly mottled or shaded with gray or brown, as in the Eurasian Wigeon, axillaries and adjacent underwing feathers in the American species are white or mostly white. These are sometimes visible and may help to confirm the female's identity.

The American Wigeon is probably most common as a breeding bird in western Canada, especially on lakes or marshes that are surrounded by brushy nesting cover or have sedge-lined meadows for alternative nesting sites. The nests are always extremely well concealed; nonetheless, they are sometimes found by crows or skunks, which are the primary egg predators. Incubation by the female requires about 24 or 25 days. Before hatching occurs, the male abandons his mate and sometimes flies considerable distances before beginning his post-breeding molt and associated month-long flightless period. Depending on geographical location, the ducklings may fledge in as little as 37 days (under the conditions of perpetual daylight and associated constant foraging in northern areas) or in as much as 48 days (in the southern parts of its range). Soon after fledging the young birds begin their fall migration.

This duck is abundant, probably numbering 1 to 2 million in recent decades.

Mary Clay/Tom Stack & Associates

Male Chiloe Wigeon

Chiloe Wigeon

(*Anas sibilatrix*)

The Chiloe Wigeon is named after Chiloe Island in southern Chile, which represents the approximate northern edge of its breeding range in southern South America. To a considerable degree, it is a lake-dwelling duck, foraging along the shoreline. Both sexes exhibit iridescent green coloration on the sides of the head (more evident in males), and both sexes have whitish cheeks and foreheads (more mottled in females).

The bright coloration of the male throughout the entire year suggests that pair-bonding is strong and fairly permanent.

Nesting occurs during the southern spring. The female seeks out a nesting site in tall grasses or weeds and deposits five to eight eggs. The male evidently remains nearby during the 26-day incubation period and rejoins his mate as soon as the ducklings have hatched. The fledging period is probably similar to that of the northern species.

No population estimates are available for this wigeon, although it is believed to be common to abundant.

Male Falcated Duck

Falcated Duck

(*Anas falcata*)

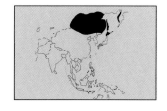

The Falcated Duck, like the Baikal Teal, is a beautiful Asian duck, which is mostly limited to eastern Siberia, China, and Japan. The male in full breeding plumage is a magnificently crested bird, with a black-and-white banded chin and throat, and an intricately scalloped black and white breast. The hindquarters are marked by a pale yellow triangle on each side of the black rump and tail coverts, and long inner flight feathers (tertials) that curve down and almost touch the water in swimming birds. The female is very similar to the female Eurasian Wigeon, but has a somewhat darker head and paler flanks.

In its behavior and feeding adaptations, the Falcated Duck is much like wigeons and the closely related Gadwall. It feeds mostly on vegetable materials obtained on the water surface, and breeds on small lakes and river oxbows that provide a mixture of open and wooded cover along their shores.

After pairing, females seek out nest sites in tall grass or brush cover and lay clutches of six to nine eggs, which they incubate for about 24 or 25 days. Males abandon their mates about the time that incubation gets well under way.

This duck is probably uncommon and declining in number. Population estimates are unavailable.

Gadwall

(Anas strepera)

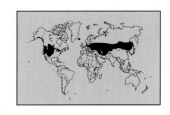

Male Gadwall

The Gadwall's lack of iridescent plumage, which sets it apart from nearly all other Northern Hemisphere dabbling ducks, has earned it the common name of Gray Duck among hunters. However, this name does not begin to suggest the subtle beauty present in the full-plumaged gray, buff, and brown male, with its two-toned brown head, delicately scalloped and penciled grayish breast and flanks, and black rump. The mostly white wing speculum is perhaps the best fieldmark for recognizing Gadwalls of either sex and in any plumage.

As their scientific name implies, Gadwalls are somewhat obstreperous during their prolonged fall-to-spring courtship period, which is marked by loud male calls (a mixture of grunts and whistles), raucous female inciting, and the usual array of male courtship display postures, especially grunt-whistles, head-up-tail-ups, and down-ups.

Pair bonds have normally been formed by the time the birds arrive on their northern prairie breeding grounds. These often consist of rather alkaline, permanent marshes, especially those having grassy islands that offer ideal nesting cover. Sometimes a colony-like nesting situation develops, with several females nesting on the same small island. No exclusive territory is maintained by the males in this case or any other. The males typically desert their mates while the latter are incubating their clutches of about ten eggs. Incubation requires about 26 days. After hatching, the ducklings are gradually moved to larger and deeper marshes for foraging during their 50-to-60-day fledging period. By the time the young have finally learned to fly, it is early autumn in central and northern Canada, and the fall migration soon begins.

Gadwall populations worldwide number in the millions.

Robert Lankinen/First Light

Baikal Teal

(Anas formosa)

Male Baikal Teal

This small Asian duck is sometimes called the Formosa Teal. The male in breeding plumage shows a distinctive combination of green, buff, black, and white on the face, including a vertical black stripe from the eye down to the black chin. By comparison, the female has an equally distinctive white stripe extending from just behind and below the eye down to the white throat, somewhat like the white marking found on a male American Wood Duck.

The Baikal Teal's breeding distribution is similar to the Falcated Duck's but is somewhat more northerly, extending to the tundra-lined shores of the Arctic Ocean in eastern Siberia. However, woodland-edged river deltas and ponds are said to be more typical summer habitats.

In these areas the bird is believed to favor foods such as small acorns as well as the seeds of soybeans, grasses, and weeds.

Males acquire their breeding plumage rather late in winter and immediately begin courtship. It is marked by distinctive single- or double-noted *ruk* calls, upward bill-tilting, and quick "burping" displays, in which the head is suddenly lifted, the small crest is raised, and the *ruk* call is uttered. Females actively incite males, and sometimes call simultaneously with the males as they display together. Once paired, the mated birds continue on to their breeding grounds.

Although this bird typically nests in grassy or shrubby cover, at times it has been found nesting in piles of driftwood or in small cavities. From six to nine eggs are laid, which are incubated by the female for about 25 days. Probably males abandon their mates before hatching has occurred, but little is yet known of the species' behavior during the nesting season.

Complete population estimates are not available for this species. Its numbers are apparently declining in its wintering area in Japan. Korea may now be its most important wintering area.

© Wayne Lynch

Green-winged Teal

(Anas crecca)

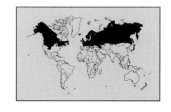

Scott Nielsen

*Male Green-winged Teal
(American race)*

The Green-winged Teal (simply called the Teal in Great Britain) is the smallest of the Eurasian species of *Anas*. It is also one of the more widespread species, ranging north to the Arctic shorelines of North America and Eurasia in summer and south to southern Mexico, equatorial Africa, and southeastern Asia in winter. In spite of this broad range, there is little geographic variation in appearance; breeding males of all races have a broad green stripe extending from the eyes back to the nape, contrasting with an otherwise rich chestnut head. Both sexes have distinctive wing speculum patterns on the secondaries, which are green inwardly and black outwardly, with a narrow white border behind and a wider one in front.

Green-winged Teal are called Krickente in Germany, perhaps in reference to their small size (12 to 15 inches/30 to 40 cm) and especially the cricket-like calls of the displaying males, which often indicate the presence of these birds even before they are seen. Groups of displaying teal remind one of battery-operated action toys, with their quick, jerky movements and animated behavior. A rapid-fire array of male displays are repeated in almost endless sequence, and aquatic displays are often interspersed with dizzying courtship chases in the air.

This tiny bird is highly susceptible to nest predators, and probably as a result the female is highly adept at hiding the nest, often under dense brushy cover. The clutch-size of eight to ten eggs is fairly large for such a small duck, and incubation lasts about 21 to 23 days. The male frequently undertakes a "molt-migration" after abandoning his mate, in order to molt in a traditionally favored area. In spite of her small size, the female defends the ducklings effectively, using overt defense as well as broken-wing tactics to lure possibly dangerous mammals away from the brood. She probably remains with her brood until they fledge in as few as 35 days in northern parts of the bird's range.

North American and Eurasian populations are generally abundant, probably numbering more than a million.

Speckled Teal

(*Anas flavirostris*)

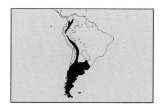

O.S. Pettingill, Jr./VIREO

Adult Speckled Teal

This small South American counterpart to the Green-winged Teal is often called the Yellow-billed Teal (as its scientific name suggests); however, some races lack yellow bills, and thus Speckled Teal is perhaps a better albeit imperfect choice. Southern Green-winged Teal might have been even better, as both sexes have wing speculum patterns that are very similar to those of the Green-winged Teal. The two species also are very similar in their vocalizations, ecology, and behavior, including nearly all the male courtship displays. Their larger size and bluish rather than yellow bills distinguish the Andean races of the Speckled Teal (sometimes called Andean Teal) from the lowland forms.

In contrast to the Northern Hemisphere teal, pair bonds in this species are quite strong and probably permanent. In conjunction with this, the male Speckled Teal lacks a dull eclipse plumage and often participates in brood-rearing. It has recently been suggested that the male makes a clear-cut decision to stay with or leave his family, for reasons that are not yet evident.

The more southern, lowland forms of Speckled Teal breed in the austral spring and summer, but the more tropically oriented, high-altitude Andean races may have quite different breeding schedules. Thus, in Venezuela the northernmost race breeds between April and September. It is even possible, although unconfirmed, that two broods per year are raised in central Chile.

The nest may be built by the female on the ground, often in dense vegetation near water or on small islands, or in elevated places, such as in the nests of Monk Parakeets or in tree-forks. There are usually five to eight eggs, and incubation lasts some 24 days.

Population estimates are not available for this species.

Cape Teal

(*Anas capensis*)

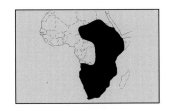

Male Cape Teal

The Cape Teal has received diverse treatment from taxonomists; Jean Delacour thought it was part of a "spotted teal" assemblage that included the superficially similar Marbled Teal, and more recently Bradley Livezey concluded that it is part of the wigeon group. However, it is difficult to imagine how people familiar with the bird in life could not fail to associate it with the green-winged teal group. It has a somewhat more flattened bill than these (but certainly not wigeon-like), and perhaps in conjunction with its pochard-like bill shape more often dives for food than do most dabbling ducks. The male also has a characteristic display involving a rapid nod-swimming over the water surface, during which it resembles a giant bug. Nevertheless, unlike wigeons and any of the so-called spotted teals, it performs the head-up-tail-up in a manner much like the Green-winged Teal and Speckled Teal. Its copulatory behavior also fits the typical pattern of the green-winged teal group.

The Cape Teal has unusually pale plumage, which together with its pale pink eyes and bill provide a distinctive, easily recognized combination of traits. It lives in often arid environments where saline pools are common and its pale colors blend into the surroundings. Pair bonds are apparently strong and possibly permanent.

The female often locates the nest on a small island, usually under thorny bushes or other protective cover. Clutch-sizes average seven or eight eggs, and incubation probably lasts about 25 or 26 days. The male actively participates in brood care, and both parents remain with the young until they fledge at about eight weeks of age.

Population estimates are not available for this species.

Gray Teal

(*Anas gibberifrons*)

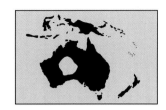

Male Gray Teal

The Gray Teal ranges from Australia, New Zealand, and much of the East Indies east to Java, although at times the Australian–New Zealand population is considered a separate species from the Indonesian one. It is highly adaptable, and in the arid interior of Australia responds rapidly to localized rainfall, which stimulates it to breed.

Courtship displays and vocalizations closely resemble those of Green-winged Teal. Unlike them, however, the male participates in brood care, and pair bonds are strong and may be permanent. Nests are usually located in elevated tree cavities near water (at least in Australia), with ground sites much less frequent. Clutches average seven or eight eggs, although dump-nesting sometimes produces much larger clutches. Incubation lasts about 27 to 29 days, and flight is attained at about 55 days. The male is normally present during the important brood-rearing period.

This duck is generally common across much of its range.

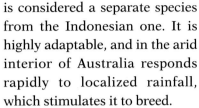Madagascan Teal

(*Anas bernieri*)

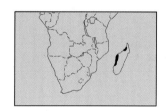

Male Madagascan Teal

This is one of three Madagascan ducks (the Meller's Duck and Madagascan White-eye are the others) that are extremely poorly known and potentially in danger of extinction before they can be saved by conservationists. The Madagascan Teal resembles the Gray Teal and may represent an offshoot from it; however, it has a velvety black speculum that lacks any kind of greenish sheen, and is also somewhat more reddish brown throughout.

Madagascan Teal have not been studied since the early 1970s, when they were observed in moderate numbers on Lake Bemamba. They were also observed during 1970 on Lake Masama, the only other large lake in this area of western Madagascar. This area is subjected to heavy sport hunting, and the species is still essentially unprotected within its tiny known range.

Chestnut Teal

(Anas castanea)

Scott Nielsen

Male Chestnut Teal

The Chestnut, or Chestnut-breasted, Teal of southern Australia bears a strong similarity to the more widely distributed Gray Teal, and they are certainly close relatives. The female Chestnut Teal is generally, but only slightly, darker than the female Gray Teal; otherwise, it is extremely similar. The male, on the other hand, has a greenish head and a richer chestnut on the breast and flanks, together with a large white area in front of the black undertail coverts. The wing speculum pattern of both sexes is nearly the same as that of the Gray Teal, namely green inwardly and black outwardly, with a narrow white border behind and a wide one in front. Although the Chestnut Teal is more likely to be found along coastlines, it also often mixes with the Gray Teal inland and probably competes with it to some degree.

Remarkably, Gray Teal and Chestnut Teal have exactly the same repertoire of courtship displays, yet seem to avoid hybridization in the wild, presumably as a result of habitat preference differences during pair-formation and the differences in male plumage. Prolonged, apparently permanent pair-bonding seems to be typical in both species, and this may also help to avoid hybridization brought on by too-hasty pair-forming behavior.

The Chestnut Teal male remains with his mate during the selection of a nest site and through the egg-laying and incubation phases. He often plays an important role in caring for the brood as well. Not surprisingly, brood success is higher in those families tended by both sexes rather than one. Clutch-sizes average eight or nine eggs, though the number is often larger as a result of dump-nesting, which is common in this cavity-nesting species. Although ground sites are sometimes used, nesting boxes or natural elevated cavities are preferred. Incubation requires about 26 days, and rearing of the young 55 to 60 days. In some cases second broods may be raised within a single breeding season.

This species is very common in southeastern Australia where it numbers in the tens of thousands.

❦Brown Teal

(*Anas aucklandica*)

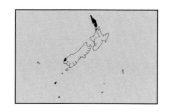

Male Brown Teal

B. Chudleigh/VIREO

The Brown Teal of New Zealand and various nearby islands appears to be a dull-colored version of the Chestnut Teal that has become isolated in these locations and modified for a rather sedentary existence. In the Auckland and Campbell Islands forms (sometimes considered full species), the birds have become semi-flightless, with reduced wings; even the New Zealand birds fly infrequently. Unlike the Chestnut Teal, the males have definite whitish eye-rings. In the New Zealand form, there is little green iridescence evident on the sides of the male's head, and in the island forms, none at all. Females also exhibit whitish eye-rings but otherwise resemble female Chestnut Teal. In both sexes the iridescent speculum pattern is rather inconspicuous.

Brown Teal are quite nocturnal and thus difficult to study, but they evidently have long-term, monogamous pair bonds. Although almost nothing is known of their social displays, because of their elusive behavior, they are evidently much like those of the Chestnut and Gray Teal. Those of the New Zealand race include several typically *Anas* displays (including head-up-tail-up, down-up, grunt-whistle, and nod-swimming). However, the head-up-tail-up and down-up are rarely performed, and social display in general is seemingly reduced compared with Gray and Chestnut Teal.

Nests of the New Zealand population are situated in clumps of sedges, or in tall grasses, rather than elevated sites. The clutch-size is rather small, averaging five or six eggs, and the incubation period is 29 or 30 days. The fledging period is about 50 to 55 days; the male remains in attendance during this critical time. Little is known of the breeding phases of the Auckland and Campbell Islands forms.

All populations of the Brown Teal are fairly rare, but this is especially so in the case of the Auckland and Campbell Islands races.

Mallard

(*Anas platyrhynchos*)

Male Mallard

Scott Nielsen

The Mallard is here broadly defined, and includes not only the North American populations that are resident along the Gulf Coast and Mexican highlands (Florida, Mottled, and Mexican Ducks) but also the island populations found on Hawaii and Laysan Island (Hawaiian Duck and Laysan Teal), all of which at various times have been classified as full species. Simple species definitions are impossible in this highly variable species, and some would even suggest that the American Black Duck might logically be included as a part of this inclusive species. In all of the just-mentioned populations, males have lost much or all of their bright breeding plumage, and in some cases (the Pacific island forms) the birds have become appreciably smaller.

These changes may be a result of inbreeding and natural selection for a sedentary life. Bright male colors and elaborate social displays are associated with intense male competition for mates in large, mobile populations.

Unlike males, females tend to be rather similar in appearance in all populations. All have wing speculum patterns that are generally iridescent blue or violet, with all-white or black and white leading and trailing borders. They also all have the usual quacking voices typical of Mallards (higher-pitched in the smaller races). During courtship, the males perform generally the same social displays, although the Pacific island ducks perform them less frequently and with less intensity.

In all the races, clutch-sizes average eight to ten eggs, and incubation typically requires about 28 days. Even in the sedentary races, the males do not participate in brood care, although it is possible that pair bonds are fairly permanent in at least some of these populations.

The typical race of the Mallard is widespread and probably numbers more than ten million birds worldwide; however, the many local races range from uncommon to rare in the case of the Hawaiian Duck and Laysan Teal.

American Black Duck

(Anas rubripes)

J.D. Taylor

Male American Black Duck

About 30 years ago, I hesitantly suggested that the American Black Duck is not a fully isolated species and that its existence might become threatened by a seemingly increasing rate of hybridization with Mallards. That prophecy has materialized at a rate that I would not have dared to suggest then, and it is now apparent that the future of the North American Black Duck as a distinct species is in jeopardy. In addition to hybridization, releases of game-farm Mallards better adapted to present-day conditions in eastern North America have tended to favor Mallards during competitive interactions, and much of the original eastern hardwood forest swampland and similar wetlands that were the Black Duck's favored nesting habitat have disappeared. Biologists and naturalists have every right to be concerned about the future of the Black Duck, which used to be the prize trophy bird of Atlantic coast hunters, and somehow seems much more beautiful and desirable than does the widely distributed, increasingly pot-bellied (from game-farm influences) Mallard.

Meller's Duck

(Anas melleri)

Paul Johnsgard

Adult Meller's Ducks

The Meller's Duck is a heavy-set Mallard-like duck of Madagascar that resembles the American Black Duck. It, too, tends to inhabit swamps, forested wetlands, and generally wooded habitats. However, its bill is somewhat longer and darker than the Black Duck's, and it has browner, less fuscous, plumage tones.

Like the Madagascan Teal and Madagascan White-eye, the Meller's Duck is endemic to and probably quite rare in Madagascar, where it once occurred rather widely in the eastern parts of that island. No definite population numbers are available, but like other Madagascan ducks it remains unprotected and could easily become endangered, if not extinct, unless efforts are made to monitor its population and protect some breeding habitats. A possibly self-introduced population probably still exists on nearby Mauritius Island, but counts in the late 1970s indicate that its numbers are also apparently pitifully small.

Yellow-billed Duck

(Anas undulata)

Male Yellow-billed Duck

The Yellow-billed Duck of Africa is the only duck of that continent having a bright yellow and black bill, and apart from the rather aberrant African Black Duck, it is the only species of the mallard group occurring there. It looks like a Meller's Duck or a North American Black Duck in body shape and general plumage pattern. In many areas, it is the most abundant duck species, occupying a variety of habitats. However, it is most common in temperate-zone regions with freshwater rather than alkaline wetlands.

Breeding often occurs after major rains, and some migratory movements are associated with local rainfall patterns. Pair-bonding patterns and courtship displays closely resemble those in Mallards.

The nest is built on the ground, usually fairly close to water, and on rare occasions may actually be floating. Apparently the male abandons his mate soon after the clutch of about six to eight eggs is laid, but little is known of this phase of the bird's breeding biology. The female incubates the eggs for 26 to 29 days and rears her brood alone. The fledging period is 65 to 70 days, and the young remain with their mother for at least six weeks after fledging.

Although complete population estimates are not available, this species is seemingly common.

Gray Duck

(Anas poecilorhyncha)

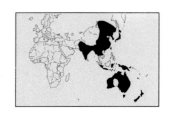

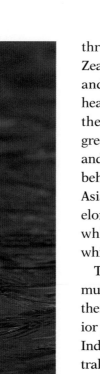

Mark K. Peck

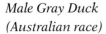

*Male Gray Duck
(Australian race)*

Like the Mallard, the Gray Duck occupies a very large range and shows considerable plumage variation throughout it. The race breeding in India has a yellow bill-tip and distinctive reddish spots at the base of the bill. Called the Spot-billed Duck, it is often considered a separate species. To the east, the progressively darker Burmese and Chinese races lack the reddish bill spots but have retained the yellow bill-tip. In the still darker races of Pacific Black Ducks, which extend from the East Indies south through Australia and New Zealand, the bill is entirely dark and the cheeks are marked by heavy blackish streaking. In all these races, the speculum is greenish, with Mallard-like black and white borders in front and behind, and in the case of the Asian races, the inner and more elongated tertials are distinctly white, forming a broad inner white border to the speculum.

The biology of Gray Ducks is much like that of Mallards, and their ecologies and social behavior patterns are also very similar. Indeed, in New Zealand and Australia, where Mallards have been introduced, hybridization between these species has blurred the genetic identity of the native Gray ("Black") Ducks. On the Mariana Islands in the western Pacific, a hybrid "swarm" of Mallards and Gray Ducks once developed naturally, but apparently has since become extinct. In Australia, the Gray Duck is perhaps still the most numerous species of duck. However, in New Zealand, hybridization and competition with Mallards has had undesirable effects on the population, and the proportion of native Gray Ducks in the combined population has declined from 95 percent in 1960 to less than 20 percent in 1985.

Male Philippine Duck

Philippine Duck

(Anas luzonica)

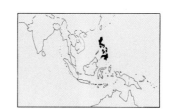

On the Philippine Islands yet another variant of the Mallard group occurs, which might logically be considered simply another race except that its plumage patterns differ substantially from the other Pacific and Asian Mallards. The distinctive tawny cinnamon head, with strong crown and eye-stripes, contrasting with an otherwise dark grayish body, allows for ready identification of both sexes. The speculum pattern resembles that of the other Mallard-like ducks. The sexes are virtually identical in appearance, and pair-bonding is perhaps more permanent than in most Mallards, given the sedentary nature of the birds as well as the infrequency of social display in captive individuals. Virtually nothing is known of the behavior of Philippine Ducks in the wild; no nests or eggs have been described from nature.

During the 1970s, this bird was known to be fairly common on several of the islands. Recently, however, its numbers have evidently declined seriously.

Male Bronze-winged Duck

Bronze-winged Duck

(Anas specularis)

The Bronze-winged, or Spectacled, Duck ranges from central Chile and northern Argentina south to Tierra del Fuego. It is especially fond of swift-flowing rivers in forested regions, but also occurs on slower rivers and ponds and lakes, particularly in wooded surroundings. The sexes are identical in appearance. In South America the birds are often called Pato perro, or dog-duck, from the barking call made by the female during inciting.

Although pair bonds in captive Bronze-winged Ducks appear to be quite strong, little is known of the species' behavior in the wild. Males respond to female inciting with chin-lifting and a repeated whistling note, but seem to lack the usual *Anas* displays, perhaps because captive observations have been mostly limited to already well-paired birds, which are less likely to exhibit such behaviors.

The few nests that have been found in the wild have been on small islets in rivers, and have been well hidden in tall grasses. Clutch-sizes are small, numbering four to six eggs, and in captivity the incubation period is about 30 days.

Population estimates are not available for this species. Its numbers are reportedly declining, and it is perhaps threatened.

Crested Duck

(*Anas specularioides*)

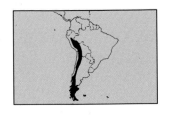

Male Crested Duck

The Crested Duck's range in South America overlaps the Bronze-winged Duck's in Patagonia. It also includes the Falkland Islands (the Patagonian race) and the Andean chain from Argentina and Chile to Bolivia and Peru (the Andean race). These two races differ slightly in appearance (the Andean race has yellow eyes, and the Patagonian race reddish eyes) as well as in their ecology. Like pintails, both types are slim-bodied and long-tailed, but have slight crests and wing speculums that resemble those of the Bronze-winged Duck. At times they have been allied with the shelducks, partly because of their rather aggressive temperament; however, both the Bronze-winged Duck and Crested Duck appear to be part of the dabbling duck group, albeit rather aberrant ones. A recent study by Bradley Livezey of the University of Kansas has confirmed this view; he regards them as representing the sister-group to the true dabbling ducks.

Crested Ducks are highly territorial birds that often live along coastlines (in the lowland form) or on mountain lakes (in the highland-adapted race). They seem to be highly carnivorous relative to most dabbling ducks. This may partly account for their aggressive nature and lack of social tendencies. The strength of the pair bond is uncertain, but it may be fairly strong, inasmuch as males have been seen attending broods in nearly all cases where family groups have been seen. Although the courtship displays of Crested Ducks are certainly *Anas*-like, they include some unusual elements, such as a highly exaggerated general shake.

The nesting season is prolonged, and the birds may have two broods each season in the Falkland Islands. Clutch-sizes number five to eight eggs, and incubation requires about 30 days. The fledging period is rather long, lasting 10 to 11 weeks.

No population estimates are available for this species, but it is seemingly common.

Northern Pintail

(*Anas acuta*)

Male Northern Pintail

This species includes three distinct races: the Northern Pintail, occurring widely throughout much of the Northern Hemisphere; and two additional races (sometimes considered separate species) that are found on the isolated Kerguelen and Crozet islands of the subantarctic waters of the Pacific Ocean. Like the Hawaiian and Laysan variants of the Mallard, these island forms are smaller and duller colored than the widespread race. They probably are small inbred populations, which have lost many of their original pintail-like traits during their periods of isolation. Northern Pintails are distinctively long-tailed and slim-bodied birds. The male in breeding plumage has an elegant brown head set off by a white stripe that starts near the nape and expands toward the rear to include the foreneck and all the underparts. Both sexes have rather inconspicuous speculum patterns, which range from bronzy or coppery green (in males) to brown (in females), bounded behind with white and in front with buffy bars. Iridescence is poorly developed or lacking in the island races.

Pintails typically renew their pair bonds annually, and have beautiful courtship ceremonies that include aerial chases as well as aquatic displays; during both the males constantly utter flute-like display calls (or "burps"). Grunt-whistles and head-up-tail-ups are also important parts of display, as is turning-the-back-of-the-head, which displays a white-bordered black nape patch.

Northern Pintails tend to be highly migratory, nesting farther north in the High Arctic than any other dabbling duck. Females there begin nesting on the tundra very early. The incubation period is a short 21 days, and at least in Alaska the young can be brought to fledging in 35 to 42 days, making possible breeding in areas having frost-free periods of only two months. During this time, the females must also complete their post-breeding molts. Then the long migration begins, occasionally to areas as far south as Colombia and Tanzania.

This duck is abundant in North America and Eurasia, numbering in the millions, but the Kerguelen and Crozet races have very small populations.

Thomas Kitchin/First Light

Male Brown Pintail

The Brown Pintail, also called the Yellow-billed Pintail, is a South American dabbling duck with a bright yellow bill and

Brown Pintail

(Anas georgica)

brown plumage in both sexes. It is widespread in much of South America; in addition, a now-extinct race once lived in the Andes of Colombia. Like the Northern Pintail, this bird tends to be common in open-country freshwater marshes, but also frequents coastal shorelines and estuarine wetlands.

The pair bond may be fairly permanent in this species, judging from the male's presence in most cases where broods have been observed.

Females lay five to seven eggs in well-hidden nests on the ground, and incubate for about 26 days, according to avicultural records. The fledging period is unknown.

No population estimates are available for the mainland birds. The South Georgia Islands population probably numbers in the low thousands.

Male White-cheeked Pintails

In South America, the White-cheeked, or Bahama, Pintail has a more northerly distribution than the Brown Pintail, and as its name implies, it also occurs in the West Indies as far north as the

White-cheeked Pintail

(Anas bahamensis)

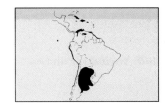

Bahamas. Another insular population (sometimes considered a full species) occurs on the Galapagos Islands. This bird seems to favor brackish or even saltwater habitats when available, although in interior South America it is also common on freshwater marshes. In Venezuela it is rather widely distributed.

The courtship display consists of repeated "burp" whistles and introductory body shakes, interspersed with a head-up-tail-up that is immediately followed by a down-up, an interesting

sequence that is unique to this pintail. Otherwise, the birds behave much like the other pintails and form what appear to be rather strong pair bonds of uncertain duration.

Clutches average six to ten eggs, and incubation by the female requires 25 days. The fledging period is unreported.

An overall population estimate is not available. The Galapagos Islands population numbers in the low thousands.

Red-billed Pintail

(Anas erythrorhyncha)

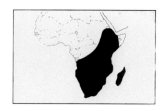

Male Red-billed Pintail

The Red-billed Pintail is often called the Red-billed Teal, and, both behaviorally and structurally, it does seem to link the pintail-like ducks with the Silver and Hottentot teal. However, my behavioral observations and Bradley Livezey's studies have grouped it clearly with the pintails rather than with these two teal. In any case, the Red-billed Pintail is rather widespread in southern and eastern Africa, and in Madagascar. It usually inhabits shallow-water areas that are rich in aquatic and shoreline vegetation. The bird is often seen dabbling in shallows or walking about on muddy flats searching for the plants and invertebrates it consumes. A social and gregarious bird, it is tolerant of other species, and in some areas quite nomadic, probably breeding whenever the aquatic food supply is most abundant.

Pair bonds are apparently not always permanent in this species, although its displays are extremely simplified, and males show no seasonal variations in plumage. Apparently some paired birds maintain long pair bonds, and others only short ones, and males only occasionally remain nearby to assist with rearing the brood. A repeated slow "burping" accompanied by considerable neck-stretching and a soft *geee* note are the only major male displays common in courting parties. Probably the combination of female inciting and turning-the-back-of-the-head by favored males serves to cement pair bonds, as it does in nearly all dabbling ducks.

Nests are built on the ground, always close to water, and clutches average ten eggs. Incubation requires 25 to 27 days, with the male sometimes joining his mate, perhaps for company or protection, while she is off the nest. About eight weeks are required to bring the young to fledging.

This pintail is a common species in Africa and probably numbers in the hundreds of thousands.

95

Silver Teal

(Anas versicolor)

Scott Nielsen

*Adult Silver Teal
(Argentine race)*

This attractive little South American duck is often and appropriately called the Versicolor Teal, presumably because of its multicolored plumage. However, Silver Teal also describes it fairly well, inasmuch as its plumage is generally silvery gray on the flanks and hindquarters, with darker vertical barring and penciling. The head is buffy to white below the eyes and dark blackish brown above, as if dark caps had been pulled down over the bird's eyes. The bill is mostly or entirely blue, although in the lowland (including the Falkland Islands) races it is yellow toward the base. The alpine-nesting Andean race is considerably larger and generally more plainly patterned throughout, but all races have a green speculum that is narrowly bounded in front with white and behind with black and white borders. The sexes are nearly identical in appearance.

Like some other South American ducks, Silver Teal have strong pair bonds. Recent observations in Argentina indicate that bi-parental brood care is well developed in this species, with eight of ten broods attended by both parents, and males showing active involvement in brood protection. Courtship displays are easily overlooked, because male vocalizations are soft rattling notes and their postures mostly limited to a slow neck-stretching "burp."

Andean race females lay rather small clutches of six or seven eggs, and their lowland counterparts lay larger ones of eight to ten eggs, usually on the ground in heavy herbaceous cover. The incubation period of both races lasts 25 or 26 days, and fledging probably requires two months or so, but little information exists on the brood-rearing phase. However, adults in wing-molt still tending broods have been seen, suggesting that parental bonds may at times be quite strong.

Population estimates are not available for this teal. It is apparently common over much of its range.

Hottentot Teal

(Anas hottentota)

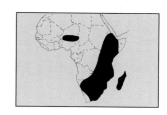

Adult Hottentot Teal

The Hottentot Teal, which is the smallest of the African *Anas* species, occurs from the equatorial belt of Africa south to the Cape, mostly in freshwater marshes edged with reeds or papyrus and containing abundant floating vegetation. In these quiet pools it inconspicuously dabbles in the evening and at night, retreating to shady and hidden sites to spend the daytime period. Its tiny size, dark brown coloration from the eyes up, lighter yellowish buff below, and a dark smudge in the ear region serve to identify the species easily. The wing speculum pattern is much like that of the Silver Teal, and indeed they are clearly very close relatives.

Like the Silver Teal, the Hottentot is quiet and undemonstrative, even during courtship display. The length and strength of its pair bonds are uncertain. Males are not known to participate in brood care even though at times they may remain with their mates well into incubation and have been seen accompanying broods (twice in 17 reported cases). Courtship displays mainly consist of the "burp" call with accompanying neck-stretching, often followed by a quick drinking action, plus a few other rather inconspicuous activities that might or might not represent ritualized signals. Even display preening occurs only rarely in this species, in spite of its well-developed iridescent speculum.

Nests are placed in cattails or similar dense cover near water, and clutches usually contain six to eight eggs. Incubation lasts 24 to 27 days, and the fledging period is unreported.

No population estimates are available for this duck. It is generally local and uncommon.

Garganey

(Anas querquedula)

Male Garganey

Garganeys (the name is said to echo the male's distinctive courtship call) form their pair bonds in their first autumn of life during active social courtship. Males have a characteristic head-throw display that accompanies their call, which sounds like the noise made by a wooden rattle. The display appears to be an exaggerated "burp" that approaches the extreme head-throws typical of many pochards, perhaps providing a clue to the evolution of such head-throws in pochards and sea ducks.

Garganeys, which are late arrivals on their breeding grounds, build their nests in tall grasses or other thick herbaceous cover. Clutches average about nine eggs, and males abandon their mates soon after incubation begins, to gather with other post-breeding drakes and unsuccessful females for molting. Incubation requires about 22 or 23 days, and fledging 30 to 35 days, with fall migration beginning soon afterward.

The Garganey is abundant in much of its range. No overall population estimates are available.

Like the Blue-winged Teal in the Old World, the Garganey undertakes extremely long migrations during the breeding season from subarctic latitudes to equatorial and even, unlike the Blue-wing, to subequatorial wintering areas as far south in Africa as Malawi. Although rare, wintering birds may reach Zimbabwe and even South Africa. It is also an early fall and late spring migrant, and occupies shallow freshwater ponds and wetlands much like those used by blue-wings in North America. Indeed, it seems to be a transitional form toward the blue-winged ducks, although its upper wing coverts are more grayish than pale blue, and its speculums are more widely bounded behind with white. However, in a recent study Bradley Livezey of the University of Kansas did not find the Garganey to be part of the blue-winged duck group; instead, he associated it with the green-winged teal, a group with which it shares few, if any, behavioral traits.

98

Blue-winged Teal

(Anas discors)

Female and male Blue-winged Teal

According to its scientific name, this is a "discordant duck," but most people would agree that it is highly attractive in voice as well as appearance. Although it is limited as a breeding bird to North America, during its long migrations it regularly reaches northern South America and has even straggled as far as Chile. The male in breeding plumage has a beautiful plum-tinted head with a crescent-shaped white patch on each cheek. In both sexes baby-blue anterior upper wing coverts are present in front of white-bordered iridescent green speculums on the secondaries. The voice of the male during display is a soft and repeated *tseeel* note. The female has the usual *Anas* quacking notes, but in keeping with her small size, they are somewhat high-pitched.

Blue-winged Teal are late spring migrants, often having traveled all the way from Central America or even northern South America. They have little time to form pair bonds once they reach their breeding areas. Probably much of the courtship occurs *en route* and consists mostly of excited neck-stretching and chin-lifting movements by males. Somewhat similar movements are used by females during inciting. All of the more elaborate male displays found in, for example, Green-winged Teal, are lacking, indicating that these two groups of teal-sized birds evolved from rather different ancestors.

Females nest under sometimes rather low grassy or sedge cover, usually along the edges of prairie ponds or marshes. They lay surprisingly large clutches of 10 or 11 eggs. Incubation lasts 21 to 23 days, and the female rears her sometimes large brood on her own. The young fledge in about 40 days, with the female starting her own flightless period at about the time her young are themselves able to fly. By then, post-breeding males are starting to regain their flying abilities, and some may have already begun to leave their breeding areas.

This bird is generally abundant, with a population in the millions.

Cinnamon Teal

(Anas cyanoptera)

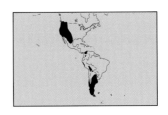

*Male Cinnamon Teal
(North American race)*

People living from the Great Plains west to the Pacific coast in North America are most likely to see this attractive little duck, although other races live in the Andes and Patagonian lowlands of South America. In the western United States, the Cinnamon Teal and the Blue-winged Teal coexist in apparent harmony, but they must compete to some degree for food, and males will even occasionally court females of the other species. The Cinnamon Teal has a slightly longer bill than the Blue-wing, and this difference, plus a generally more rusty plumage, often helps to identify it correctly in the field. The upper wing patterns of both sexes are exactly like the Blue-winged Teal's, associating it not only with that duck but also with the several species of shovelers. A close look at the Cinnamon Teal's long and slightly "droop-tipped" bill shows this ancestral affinity, too.

The Cinnamon Teal seems to be most abundant on the rather alkaline shallow marshes of the western inter-mountain plains, where saltgrass cover provides it with sometimes limited nesting protection. For this reason, islands having high grassy cover are preferred for nesting sites. The male occasionally abandons his mate about the time that the clutch of nine or ten eggs is completed. However, because of frequent renesting following clutch loss, a male that has remained nearby may be able to refertilize the female for a second or even third nesting attempt. Incubation lasts 23 to 25 days, and 35 days are needed to bring the young to fledging. The first fall flights out of the breeding grounds are by adult males, followed within a month by post-breeding females and young birds.

The North American Cinnamon Teal population numbers several hundred thousand. Although no estimates exist for the populations that live farther south, it is believed that the Colombian population may be endangered.

Thomas Kitchin

100

Red Shoveler

(*Anas platalea*)

Male Red Shoveler

This South American species of shoveler has a reddish-toned and dark-spotted male plumage that resembles the Cinnamon Teal's, and its bill is also perhaps slightly less modified for filter-feeding than those of the other three species. It is somewhat larger than the Cinnamon Teal, and the male has distinctive yellowish eyes and a rather pale head. The female, on the other hand, closely resembles the female Cinnamon Teal in plumage pattern and color. Although its range overlaps the teal's, it seems to prefer brackish waters and coastal lagoons to freshwater habitats. This bird is an effective filter-feeder, consuming plankton-sized materials and probably some larger foods, and is the only true shoveler species breeding in South America.

Pair bonds, which are evidently rather strong, are rapidly formed or re-formed in fall flocks. Recently in Argentina, males were observed accompanying their broods in only 5 out of 26 families. In at least some of these cases, the attending males showed no clear evidence of providing any parental care.

A major male courtship display of this species, as well as other shovelers, is mock-feeding, which Red Shovelers perform immediately after uttering soft *tooka* notes that probably attract the female's attention. Males also perform chin-lifting as a hostile display toward competing drakes. By comparison, the mutual head-pumping that precedes copulation is done with the bill held level or tilted slightly downward.

Females nest in grassy vegetation and lay clutches of five to eight eggs, which they incubate for about 25 days. The fledging period is unreported but is probably similar to that of other shovelers.

No overall population estimates are available for this species. It is apparently rather common.

© Wayne Lynch

Male Cape Shoveler

This African duck is the only species of shoveler breeding on that continent (Northern Shovelers sometimes winter south to the equator). Rather surprisingly, it has a restricted distribution

Cape Shoveler

(*Anas smithii*)

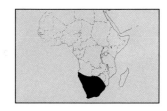

centering on South Africa. It is darker and browner in plumage tone than the Red Shoveler, but the male's eyes are also pale yellow, and the otherwise similar female has brown eyes. The bird seems to exhibit seasonal monogamy, with only a slight tendency for previously mated birds to reform their pair bonds.

The social displays of the Cape Shoveler are very much like those of the other blue-winged ducks, with mock-feeding and

accompanying "wooden" male calls being especially evident.

Like other shovelers, the nests are placed in fairly low herbaceous cover. Clutches average nine or ten eggs. Males may remain near their mates through the egg-laying period but leave soon afterward to begin their molt. Incubation takes 27 or 28 days, and fledging requires eight weeks.

No population estimates are available.

Male Australasian Shoveler

This species of Australia and New Zealand exhibits a rather strange assortment of male plumage traits that recalls both the Blue-winged Teal (the white facial crescent) and the Northern Shoveler (the rusty flanks and pale breast). Some molting Northern Shoveler males closely

Australasian Shoveler

(*Anas rhynchotis*)

resemble the Australasian Shoveler male when it is approaching its breeding condition, suggesting not only that these two species are closely related but also that the white facial markings are probably an ancestral trait of the blue-winged ducks and do not suggest any particularly close affinity between the Blue-winged Teal and this species. Apart from these minor plumage differences, the ecologies and behaviors of the Australasian Shoveler and the Northern Shoveler appear to be very similar.

The male courtship displays are

much like those of the other shovelers, with hostile chin-lifting directed toward rivals and much ritualized or "mock" feeding.

The nest is usually built on the ground, but at times in hollow stumps, and typically contains 9 to 11 eggs. Incubation probably lasts 24 or 25 days, and the young reportedly fledge in about eight to ten weeks, a very long fledging period.

The Australian population is unknown but probably declining; the New Zealand population numbers about 100,000 to 150,000 and is stable.

Northern Shoveler

(Anas clypeata)

Male Northern Shoveler

This is by far the most widely distributed and abundant of all the shoveler species. The male also happens to be the most brilliantly colored, with an all-green iridescent head, white breast, and rusty brown flanks. Like the other shovelers, the male has yellow eyes, whereas the female has dark brown eyes and the usual barred and scalloped brown-and-buff plumage pattern of nearly all female dabbling ducks. The Northern Shoveler is highly migratory, moving almost as far south in winter as the Blue-winged Teal. Like the teal, it is a rather tardy spring migrant. By the time it returns to the American and Canadian prairies, it is in prime breeding plumage and usually already paired.

Unlike many *Anas* species, the male Northern Shoveler may defend a definite breeding territory. This may be important because its food supply of planktonic life is highly specialized. Like the other shovelers, ritualized or "mock" feeding, hostile chin-lifting, and short jump-flights by males are primary elements of social display. Probably few pair bonds persist between breeding seasons in this highly migratory species, and the male shows no interest in helping to look after the brood, although at times he may remain with his mate until the young hatch or even slightly beyond.

Clutch-sizes average ten eggs, and incubation has been estimated to last anywhere from 21 to 28 days. Fledging has been judged to require from as few as 36 days in northern parts of the breeding range to as many as 60 days farther south, where daily feeding opportunities are substantially limited because of shorter summer days.

The total world population of this widespread species numbers in the millions.

103

❧ Marbled Teal

(*Marmaronetta angustirostris*)

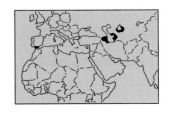

Scott Nielsen

*Male and female
Marbled Teal*

Until my behavioral studies a few decades ago, the Marbled Teal was thought to be simply another of the so-called spotted teal. However, my behavioral and anatomical observations pointed out that the species represents an important transitional form that helps to link the dabbling ducks with the pochards, and subsequent researchers have generally confirmed that finding. Bradley Livezey's studies at the University of Kansas placed it near the pochards as a sister-genus to that group. Like pochards, this spotted, grayish buff duck lacks an iridescent speculum pattern.

Pair bonds are apparently reformed each fall, during a prolonged period of social display marked by a unique array of pair-forming displays in both sexes that bear few similarities to typical *Anas* species. In their copulatory behavior, the birds are even more divergent, and both their precopulatory and postcopulatory displays have many elements in common with pochards. Like pochards, Marbled Teal dive surprisingly well considering that their hind toes are not strongly lobed.

Their nesting biology in the wild is little known, but in captivity females lay clutches of 10 or 11 eggs, which require about 25 days of incubation. The male apparently abandons his mate rather early in the breeding cycle, and the female thus rears the young entirely on her own.

The species has a restricted and now seriously declining range, which extends from northeastern Africa to the Middle East, with some birds ranging in winter east to Pakistan. Few, if any, conservation efforts are under way in the species' major breeding range.

Pochards

Scott Nielsen

Male Ring-necked Duck

THE POCHARDS ARE A WELL-DEFINED AND FAIRLY EASILY RECOGNIZED group of diving ducks. In North America, they are often called bay ducks or inland divers. All the species are adept at diving, with feet that are placed somewhat to the rear of the body (for better underwater maneuvering) and rather heavy bodies compared with the dabbling ducks. For these reasons, pochards take flight with difficulty, typically running along the water surface for some distance before becoming airborne. Once aloft, they fly rapidly but with little apparent ability to engage in evasive aerial maneuvers. The birds tend to favor large, open waters of a depth that allows them to reach underwater plants, such as pondweeds, or the often silty or muddy bottoms where they can find invertebrate foods in abundance. They always lack iridescent colors on their wings, and few show any iridescence elsewhere, although purplish to greenish sheens may be apparent in good light on the heads of some breeding-plumaged males.

Red-crested Pochard

(*Netta rufina*)

Male Red-crested Pochard

The male Red-crested Pochard reminds me of a shaving brush; its head feathers form a bushy crest of flaming orange-red, set off with black on the lower hind-neck and breast and white on the flanks. The eyes, bill, and feet are also reddish orange. The female is less gaudy, with a distinctly two-toned (dark above, whitish below) head color and brown rather than reddish eyes and feet. Like the male, the female has conspicuous white wing stripes extending from the inner secondaries to the outer primaries. The

Red-crested Pochard is one of the so-called narrow-billed pochards. Its narrow, straight bill is somewhat like those of the *Anas*, rather than the flattened and broader bills of most pochards, especially the scaups. This bird has a wide albeit scattered breeding distribution from Spain east to former south-central Soviet Asia, and it prefers a warm-temperate climate.

The Red-crested Pochard is seemingly unique among ducks in that, during pair formation, the male "courtship-feeds" the

female. This is perhaps a slight overstatement; often the water-logged twigs and other materials brought to the female are inedible, but nonetheless she accepts them in her bill. A major male display during social courtship is a sneeze-like movement and call, during which the male's head is slightly turned and tilted toward the female that he is courting. Neck-stretching and a movement of the head and bill forward over the water while uttering a nasal call resemble the displays of typical pochards, although a head-throw movement is lacking (unless it is represented in vestigial form by the sneeze display). The female incites in rather *Anas*-like fashion, and precopulatory behavior is an interesting mixture of *Anas*- and *Aythya*-like posturing.

At least in the former USSR the birds have paired by their arrival on the nesting grounds, and females soon lay a clutch of eight to ten eggs, which they incubate for 26 to 28 days. The males do not participate in brood-rearing, which requires a fairly long period of 10 to 11 weeks before fledging by the young birds.

There are no overall population estimates for this duck, but it is seemingly more abundant in the eastern part of its range.

Scott Nielsen

Southern Pochard

(Netta erythrophthalma)

Male Southern Pochard

This is the only species of narrow-billed pochard to occur in both the warmer parts of South America and eastern and southern portions of Africa (where it is sometimes called the African Pochard). These two populations are usually regarded as distinct races; the birds from Africa are slightly paler and more brownish than those from South America. Males are mostly dark-colored, with blackish head, breast, and back coloration, red eyes, and rich brown flanks. Females are mostly various shades of brown but have white on the chin, cheeks, and sides of the head. Like the other so-called narrow-billed pochards, this species has a rather narrow, long bill; the birds forage by diving, upending in shallow water, and at times even feeding while standing at the water's edge.

Although the female's inciting notes are harsh-sounding, the primary courtship call of the male is a very soft *aeerooow*, which reminds one of the rapid unwinding of a spring. This call is uttered during head-throw and head-retraction displays; additionally, the male performs inconspicuous "sneak" displays with the bill directed toward a female while he utters a soft multi-note call. Pair bonds appear to be transitory, at least in captive conditions, although there are accounts of males apparently attending broods, or at least associating with brood-tending females.

Like many tropically oriented ducks, the nesting season of this species is varied, but in general seems to be associated with the wet season. The female may build the nest on fairly dry ground or in emergent vegetation over water. The clutch averages nine eggs, and the incubation period lasts about 26 days (some estimates of 20 or 21 days exist). Fledging time is undetermined.

The South American population is now limited in distribution (perhaps restricted to southeastern Brazil) and has apparently disappeared from most of its earlier range in northwestern and western South America.

Rosybill

(Netta peposaca)

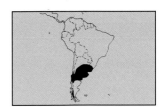

Male Rosybill

The Rosybill (or Rosy-billed Pochard) is an attractive diving duck that is common over many parts of southeastern South America. The male has a brilliant red bill that is inflated at the base, contrasting with a black head, breast, and back, and with gray flanks and a white patch under the tail. Conspicuous white wing stripes are evident only in flight. The female closely resembles the female Southern Pochard, but the white on the side of the head is more mottled, making the head less clearly two-toned. The species is found on warm lowland marshes and lakes from northern Argentina north to southern Brazil. It probably dives in shallow waters for its food; however, its diet in nature remains to be studied.

Pair bonds appear to be temporary; there are no accounts of males helping to rear the young. Courtship is marked by conspicuous displays on the part of both sexes. Males as well as females perform an exaggerated drinking movement as a greeting display, and both sexes perform sneaking displays in which the head and neck are extended over the water and directed toward the potential mate. Only occasionally do males perform head-throws, but both sexes use mock-preening displays.

The female tends to build the nest over water rather than on land, and also tends to dump its eggs in the nests of other species. In turn, its nest is often "parasitized" through the addition of eggs laid by Black-headed Ducks. Incubation lasts about 28 days (compared with 21 days for the Black-headed Ducks, whose highly precocial ducklings thus hatch about a week before any of their host's eggs). After hatching, broods often amalgamate, and female Rosybills tending large numbers of young have at times been seen.

Scott Nielsen

108

Canvasback

(Aythya valisineria)

Male Canvasback

Thomas Kitchin

The Canvasback is one of the most distinctive of all North American ducks, and the one most highly prized by hunters. It is the largest of the pochards, and both sexes have long, sloping bills that give them a regal appearance. The whitish gray (canvas-colored) back and flank coloration of the male is also distinctive, and in winter plumage the female likewise has paler grayish sides and back than do any of the other pochard species. Limited to North America, this bird is most common on the tule- and cattail-lined prairie marshes of the northern plains, but locally extends its nesting distribution all the way to the Arctic Ocean and Bering Sea. It is mostly vegetarian, with pondweeds, water lilies, and wild celery among its favorite freshwater foods. In winter it concentrates on estuaries where eelgrass and wigeon grass grow abundantly.

Pair bonds are renewed annually, and courtship is marked by prolonged periods of both aquatic and aerial displays, including exciting chases and occasional dives. The major male courtship call is a soft dove-like note, which is used during the head-throw and also during the "kinked-neck" posture. Males also perform a lowered head posture, the sneak, in which the bill is directed toward potential mates. On their breeding grounds the birds occupy rather large home ranges, with little or no territorial aggression evident between nearby pairs.

The female constructs its partly floating nest in dense beds of emergent vegetation. It needs such stable-water habitats, along with nearby areas of open water for foraging and easy take-offs and landings, for successful breeding. In some areas raccoons, skunks, and various other avian egg predators cause serious losses each year. Incubation of the nine or ten eggs requires 24 or 25 days, and fledging 60 to 70 days, during which time the female may begin her own molting period and abandon her young before they have fledged.

The population of Canvasbacks has been declining in recent decades as a result of breeding habitat losses. It probably numbers a few hundred thousand.

Eurasian Pochard

(*Aythya ferina*)

Male Eurasian Pochard

This is the "Common" Pochard of Europe, which to North American observers resembles a hybrid between the Canvasback and Redhead, for both sexes have a bill shape, head shape, and plumage patterns that are generally intermediate between these two types. All three species forage in rather deep, open waters, mostly for vegetable materials. They also are quite similar in their vocalizations, pair-forming displays, and breeding. Furthermore, they are all dependent on permanent to semi-permanent marshes in cool-temperate to subarctic climates.

On their breeding grounds, the females seek out nest sites, usually among dense reed beds or other emergent vegetation, but at times on muddy areas along the shore if dense vegetation is lacking. Clutch-sizes are rather small—six to nine eggs. The incubation period lasts 24 to 28 days, and fledging requires 50 to 55 days.

The population of this fairly common species probably approaches a million birds.

Redhead

(*Aythya americana*)

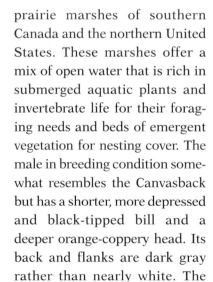

Female and male Redheads

Like the Canvasback, Ring-necked Duck, and Lesser Scaup, the Redhead is exclusively a North American species of pochard. Its breeding range, which overlaps with those of the other three, centers on the prairie marshes of southern Canada and the northern United States. These marshes offer a mix of open water that is rich in submerged aquatic plants and invertebrate life for their foraging needs and beds of emergent vegetation for nesting cover. The male in breeding condition somewhat resembles the Canvasback but has a shorter, more depressed and black-tipped bill and a deeper orange-coppery head. Its back and flanks are dark gray rather than nearly white. The female is harder to distinguish, but its plumage is brownish rather than grayish on its body, and it has a lighter eye-ring and eye-stripe.

Some females (perhaps as many as half) lay eggs "parasitically" in the nests of other ducks; however, the hatching success of these eggs is low. Among non-parasitic females, the average clutch-size seems to be seven or eight eggs, and incubation requires 24 to 28 days. Fledging of the young requires 55 to 75 days.

During the 1970s, the population exceeded half a million birds; for the past few decades it has been declining.

Ring-necked Duck

(Aythya collaris)

*Female and male
Ring-necked Ducks*

The Ring-necked Duck, or Ring-bill as it is commonly and appropriately called by most hunters, is another native North American pochard. Its range is centered in central and eastern Canada. In some ways it is rather scaup-like in appearance (males are mostly black with white flanks), but an examination of the plumages of females and ducklings immediately shows that the species is a typical pochard. Like the other typical pochards, both sexes have gray rather than white wing stripes; however, the male's bill is more strongly banded with gray, white, and black than any of the other pochards' bills. The female is a rather nondescript grayish brown, usually with a well-defined whitish eye-ring and eye-stripe and fainter banding evident on the bill.

Unlike the other American pochards, this species inhabits forested swamps, bogs, and similar often acidic wetlands of eastern Canada, although it extends locally to British Columbia. The birds form pair bonds as yearlings and thereafter apparently re-form their bonds annually. Courtship takes much the same form as in the other pochards, although it is visually inconspicuous and the associated vocalizations are rather weak.

On their breeding grounds, females seek out islands, small mats of floating vegetation, and similar sites for their nests, but occasionally nest on dry sites. Incubation requires 26 to 27 days, and fledging about seven to eight weeks.

Unlike Canvasbacks and Redheads, the population of this species has increased in recent decades and may now number close to a million birds.

Male Australasian White-eyes

Australian hunters and birders call this species the Hardhead, an unattractive name with no logical basis. This bird is one of the group of white-eyed pochards

Australasian White-eye

(*Aythya australis*)

in which males have whitish eyes, generally brownish plumage with little or no iridescence, and white wing stripes. The white-eyes are near relatives of the typical pochards and, like them, have primarily vegetarian diets. This species mainly inhabits permanent marshes across much of Australia, Tasmania, and southwestern New Guinea. At one time it also bred in New Zealand, but now occurs there only as a vagrant.

Australasian White-eyes form pair bonds annually. The birds

mostly breed on permanent wetlands in southeastern Australia, where courtship is marked by strong head-throws, kinked-neck postures, and sneak displays.

Females build their nests in dense emergent vegetation and at times on land, or even on tree stumps. Their clutches average 9 to 13 eggs, and incubation probably lasts about 25 days, although it has been reported as 30 to 32 days. Little information on the brood-rearing phase exists.

No overall population estimates are available.

Male Siberian White-eye

This species is commonly called Baer's Pochard, a name that tends to make incorrect associations between it and the typical

Siberian White-eye

(*Aythya baeri*)

pochards. Except for its dark and slightly iridescent male head plumage, the Siberian White-eye is clearly a typical member of the white-eye group. It has a restricted breeding range in eastern Siberia, essentially replacing the Ferruginous White-eye there, and at times has been regarded as only a well-marked subspecies of that duck. However, it is in many ways intermediate between the Ferruginous and Australasian white-eyes and is clearly a distinct species.

The Siberian White-eye is very little studied in the wild, but observations of captive birds indicate that it differs only slightly from Ferruginous and especially Australasian white-eyes. The nest and its clutch of about ten eggs are said to be placed along lake shorelines or the banks of streams. Virtually no other information exists.

This duck may be rare and its numbers declining. No overall population estimates are available.

Male Ferruginous White-eye

Ferruginous White-eye

(Aythya nyroca)

The Ferruginous White-eye is the best studied and most widely distributed of all the white-eye group. Its breeding range extends from western Europe (where it is somewhat rare) and northwestern Africa (where it once bred but may now be only a winter migrant) east to central China. Perhaps the heart of its breeding range is now in the western parts of the former USSR. The bird inhabits shallow pools and ponds having extensive reed beds and requires less open water than do some of the pochard species. It forages predominantly for plant materials (including leafy parts, roots, and seeds); invertebrates make up only a very small percentage of its food.

Pair bonds are re-established each year, through a prolonged period of social display. Females are actively involved in stimulating and participating in this display activity, and males often swim about in a rather jerky manner, raising their crown feathers into a triangular crest, depressing their tails, and performing such displays as head-throws, kinked-neck postures, and sneak postures, often in rapid succession.

At least in the former USSR, the nests are placed in reed beds or other emergent vegetation on islands or along the edges of ponds or rivers. Clutches number 7 to 11 eggs, incubation requires about 25 to 27 days, and fledging of the young occurs 55 to 60 days after hatching.

Total population estimates are unavailable, but the population probably numbers more than 100,000, mostly in former Soviet regions.

Male Madagascan White-eye

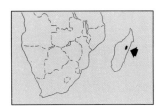

❂Madagascan White-eye

(Aythya innotata)

This extremely little known species of white-eye is native to a few lakes of eastern Madagascar, especially the island's largest, Lake Alaotra. In the early parts of this century, this shallow and papyrus-lined lake supported a large population of these white-eyes. However, in the past few decades, the lake has been greatly affected by silting, burning of the papyrus edge vegetation, and uncontrolled hunting, as well as the introduction of exotic fishes. All recent efforts to find this duck on Lake Alaotra have failed, although there is a slight chance that it may survive on smaller lakes in the region. It is highly endangered

Male Tufted Duck

The Tufted Duck might have been better called the Tufted Scaup, inasmuch as it seems to have its strongest affinities with the scaup-like ducks rather than, for example, the Ring-necked Duck, with which it has at times been confused and often allied

Tufted Duck

(Aythya fuligula)

taxonomically. If it were not for the male's dangling crest and dark back, it would be difficult to distinguish it from most scaups. The female is also very scaup-like. The Tufted Duck has the broadest distribution of any of the scaups, ranging from Iceland to the Kamchatka Peninsula and Japan and wintering south almost to equatorial Africa. It dives for insect larvae, mollusks and crustaceans in freshwater as well as coastal habitats.

Pair bonds, which begin to form during the first winter of life, are renewed annually during extended periods of social courtship. Like other scaups, the male displays of Tufted Ducks tend to be performed rapidly, and can be easily overlooked.

Females build their nests on the ground, on islands when they are available, and frequently among colonies of gulls or terns, whose colonial defensive behavior offers some protection from jackdaws and other predators. Clutch-sizes average ten eggs, and incubation lasts about 24 days. The young are fledged in 45 to 50 days.

This species is generally abundant, although no total population estimates are available.

Male New Zealand Scaup

The New Zealand Scaup occurs on both major islands of New Zealand. It is the darkest in overall plumage of all the pochards (in New Zealand it is often called

❂New Zealand Scaup

(Aythya novaeseelandiae)

the Black Teal). Males have contrasting yellow eyes, and females have white cheek patches between their eyes and bill.

Because of its rarity, it has not been well studied in the wild, but is known to consume a mixture of invertebrates and some plant foods. Pair-bonding behavior is also unstudied. Captive birds, however, seem to be little if at all different from the other scaups in their courtship behaviors and

pair-bonding tendencies.

Nests are placed near water, often in sedge clumps, and clutches consist of six or seven eggs. Incubation lasts 28 to 30 days, and fledging probably requires about 75 days.

This rare duck was much more common before European settlement, and seems to be increasing, albeit slowly. It is fully protected and probably numbers 5,000 to 10,000.

Lesser Scaup

(Aythya affinis)

Male Lesser Scaup

The birds form pair bonds annually, mostly while in wintering areas or during spring migration, but display activities are very hard to detect at any distance, owing to the soft calls of the males and their very rapid displays. The head-throw is especially fast and is nothing more than a blur to human eyes, accompanied by a soft *wheee-ooo* note. Although yearling females pair and may attempt to nest, only a small number of them are successful in rearing young at that age.

Nests are built on dry sites often within about 50 yards (45 m) of water, and in herbaceous cover. This bird frequently chooses to nest on islands, especially those supporting colonies of gulls or terns, apparently for protection. Clutches average ten eggs, and incubation requires about 23 to 25 days. The fledging period is 45 to 50 days, with females often deserting their brood as fledging approaches so that they can undergo their flightless molting period.

The scaups are the most abundant pochards in North America. In recent decades the combined populations of Lesser and Greater scaups have numbered between 5 and 10 million birds, of which the Lesser Scaup has contributed all but about a half-million.

This species is the so-called Little Blue-bill of North American hunters. It is slightly smaller than the Greater Scaup, is more inclined to occur on shallower and smaller water areas, and is generally more associated with freshwater habitats during the non-breeding season. The male differs from the Greater Scaup male in several ways. Its head profile is higher and slightly crested, the head has a purplish rather than greenish sheen, and the white wing stripe does not extend so far out on the flight feathers, typically terminating on the secondaries. Likewise, the female closely resembles the female Greater Scaup, but its wing stripes are also shorter, and it has a somewhat less extensive white patch on the cheeks between the eyes and the bill.

115

Greater Scaup

(Aythya marila)

A group of Greater Scaups

Thomas Kitchin

The Greater Scaup has a much more widespread range than does the Lesser Scaup, occurring in both North America and Eurasia. The differences in appearance between the species are mentioned in the Lesser Scaup account. One major ecological difference is that Greater Scaups nest at more northerly latitudes than Lessers and winter more often in coastal locations. When Greater Scaups do occur in inland areas, they are found on larger and deeper bodies of water than are Lessers. Both feed heavily on invertebrates, especially mollusks in the case of the Greaters, and a combination of small mollusks, crustaceans, and aquatic insects in the case of the Lessers.

Most of the North American population of Greater Scaups nest in Alaska, especially on coastal tundra, with smaller numbers breeding in northwestern Canada. Strangely, the primary wintering area is on the Atlantic coast rather than the Pacific coast, so a transcontinental migration across Canada must be undertaken twice a year.

This bird nests close to water, often in rather tall tundra grasses, and lays 7 to 11 eggs. The incubation period lasts 24 or 25 days, and the male does not help care for the brood.

Sea Ducks

Robert Lankinen/First Light

*Female Common Merganser
with young*

THE SEA DUCKS COMPRISE A LARGE AND DIVERSE GROUP OF DIVING DUCKS. At first glance, they do not seem to have much in common, other than that they tend to winter on salt water and often breed in coastal tundra or temperate-zone forests, especially those of the Northern Hemisphere. The largest and more bulky of the sea ducks are the eiders, which are mostly mussel-eating ducks of the arctic tundra zone with broad bills designed for crushing shells. Among the smallest and most streamlined of the sea ducks are the mergansers, which mostly catch fish in open pursuit, and whose narrow bills are long and cormorant-like, with a recurved nail at the tip and saw-like edges. Between these two extremes are such birds as the scoters, goldeneyes, and a few other species, which are also predatory diving ducks but which forage on a great variety of food types.

Apparently all of the sea ducks, even the smallest species, require two years to become sexually mature and sometimes even longer to attain their adult plumages. Many of the sea ducks (especially the mergansers and goldeneyes) are cavity-nesters, using elevated tree cavities or, less commonly, ground cavities. These birds somewhat resemble perching ducks in that they tend to have long and broad tails, but apart from such adaptive similarities there is no reason to believe that they are closely related. Some people have also speculated that the sea ducks, and especially the eiders, evolved from ancestral dabbling ducks, but my own behavioral observations as well as other studies have supported the view that they emerged from ancestral diving ducks. Bradley Livezey's study suggested a relationship with the stifftails, whereas my observations favor a more generalized affinity with several diving duck groups, including the pochards.

Common Eider

(Somateria mollissima)

Fred Bruemmer

Male and female Common Eiders

The Common Eider, or simply Eider, is a widely ranging species whose various populations encircle the globe at high latitudes. These numerous populations vary somewhat in size and plumage. The Pacific Eider is the largest and most distinctive, and occasionally is regarded as a separate species. Generally the birds weigh 3 to 5 pounds (1 to 2 kg). The male has a black-and-white plumage pattern that includes a black crown, white cheeks, greenish yellow sides of the head, and an all-white back and breast. The female is strongly vertically barred with tones of brownish buff and blackish brown, in an overall pattern slightly resembling that of female Mallards. First-year males and males in eclipse tend to be blackish rather than closely resembling the adult female. In both sexes and all races, the feathers on the sides of the cheeks extend forward, almost reaching the rear edge of the nostrils.

Like other larger eider species, males of this species have a variety of cooing calls that are used during social courtship and are accompanied by various head movements. These differ slightly among the races, but these races are all more similar to one another in their displays than any is to, for example, the King Eider. Much time is spent during spring in social courtship display, with the females actively inciting and the males responding with their several cooing postures and calls. These same calls and postures are used by males in the precopulatory situation, which is quite different from the mutual and unique precopulatory displays of dabbling ducks and pochards.

Females lay rather small clutches of four or five eggs (early clutches are larger than later ones, and those of middle latitudes are larger than extreme northern or southern ones). Incubation lasts about 25 to 30 days, and fledging requires about eight weeks. Eiders often nest colonially, and the young of many females frequently merge to form large crèches, which are attended by several females.

Overall estimates for all races of this duck are not available, but it numbers in the millions in both North America and Eurasia.

King Eider

(Somateria spectabilis)

Male King Eider

The King Eider is well named; the male in breeding plumage has a magnificent bluish hood that is capped in front by a bright orange-red knob extending from the forehead to the nostrils and outlined in black. The eyes are also outlined from below in black, and in contrast to the Common Eider and Spectacled Eider, the back plumage is likewise black. The male has curious sail-like tertial feathers rising from his inner wings, which unlike those of the Mandarin are constantly held aloft as the male is swimming. The female has a contrasting dark and light brown plumage somewhat like that of the Common Eider, but the markings are more crescent-shaped rather than tending toward vertical barring. In both sexes, the feathers of the cheeks do not reach as far forward as in the Common Eider. As in that species, males in eclipse and first-year males tend to be blackish in color, rather than resembling the brown females.

Like Common Eiders, King Eiders have nearly circumpolar breeding ranges, although they don't normally breed in Scandinavia or Iceland. Their courtship calls and vocalizations also recall those of Common Eiders, and these two similar species have been reported to hybridize occasionally. It is not long between the time that a female is mated and the start of the egg-laying season, which occurs as soon as coastal tundra areas begin to become snow-free.

Eggs are laid in dry-land nests, sometimes a quarter mile (0.5 km) or more from water. As soon as egg-laying is finished, the males begin to head back to sea, often moving to common molting areas a considerable distance away. The clutch of about five eggs is incubated for 22 to 24 days, and the young probably require seven to eight weeks to fledge.

Overall estimates are not available for this species, but it numbers in the millions in both North America and Eurasia.

Roger Tidman/NHPA

Spectacled Eider

(Somateria fischeri)

Male Spectacled Eider

The Spectacled Eider is perfectly named: the white (in males) or buff (in females) patches that surround the eyes are the most conspicuous of the species' field-marks and provide for instant identification. The male's pale, blue-edged eyes, shaggy golden-green hood, and black lower breast are also distinctive among eiders. The male in eclipse plumage is somewhat blackish in tone, like the other eiders, and at all ages and in both sexes the feathering on the upper half of the bill extends forward almost to reach the nostrils. The Specta-cled Eider has the smallest breed-ing range of all the eiders, and is largely limited to the coastlines of the Bering Sea and adjoining Arc-tic Ocean of eastern Siberia and northern Alaska. Its wintering area remains a mystery, although it is assumed that it winters at sea somewhere in the vicinity of the Aleutian Islands.

Although observations of this species are rather limited, it is likely that courtship display begins at sea, and it is known that it continues until the birds arrive at their breeding grounds in late May. Displays of the males are a mixture of calls and pos-tures that clearly relate to those of the two other larger eiders, as well as some that are otherwise found only in the small Steller's Eider. In contrast to all the other eiders, the male's vocalizations are so soft as to be essentially inaudible to human ears beyond about 20 yards (18 m).

The female begins nesting on the coastal tundra as soon as it is partly snow-free, and lays a clutch of about five eggs. Incuba-tion requires 24 days, and the young are led to coastal edges as soon as they are able to travel. Fledging probably requires about 50 days, and soon there-after the birds leave the breeding grounds, presumably for still-undiscovered autumn staging or wintering areas.

There are probably about 200,000 breeding birds, mainly in Siberia.

Steller's Eider

(Polysticta stelleri)

Male Steller's Eider

J.P. Myers/VIREO

breast, a black neck-stripe, and black edging around the eyes and greenish nape. The female is a dark, chunky duck somewhat recalling the Brown Teal in both general color and body shape; however, in common with the male, it has bluish and white-edged iridescent speculum patterns. Eclipse-plumage males are somewhat more dusky-toned than the females.

Steller's Eiders are gregarious birds, and during social display in spring often engage in active courtship. One of the most spectacular of the male's displays is called rearing, and consists of a sudden, silent throwing back of the entire body in the water, momentarily exposing the brownish underparts, and just as quickly dropping back and hiding them. Other displays are associated with precopulatory activity, particularly the alternation of preening and drinking sequences by the male as the female lies prone and watches intently.

Nests are built along coastal tundra, and clutches of seven to eight eggs are typical. The incubation period is unknown, as is the fledging period.

No detailed estimates are available, though there are probably close to 500,000 of these ducks.

This small eider has a range only slightly larger than that of the Spectacled Eider, and both are mostly centered around the Bering Sea. In this species wintering is known to occur along the Kamchatka Peninsula as well as the Aleutian Islands, with birds also occasionally moving east to winter along the coasts of Scandinavia. The male in breeding plumage can be easily recognized by its mostly white head, tawny-rufous breast, and unique iridescent striping along the back produced by ornamental scapulars. It also has a strange black spot on each side of the

Harlequin Duck

(*Histrionicus histrionicus*)

Male and female Harlequin Ducks

The Harlequin Ducks might well be regarded as the most beautiful of North American waterfowl, at least by those persons who are not overwhelmed by the iridescent magnificence of the American Wood Duck. The Harlequin has a more subdued beauty, with only a slight bluish iridescence, mainly on the secondaries. Its elegant combination of indigo, black, white, and chestnut is organized in a complicated "harlequin" pattern. The female is mostly dark brown, with white patches around the ears and on the front of the face. This duck seems to be completely at home either in the fast white-water of mountain streams or among crashing coastal breakers, where it feeds on the invertebrates associated with the rocky bottoms of these specialized habitats. It flies infrequently, and in spite of the bright coloration of the male, it is often very hard to locate in its blue-water, white-foam surroundings.

Harlequin Ducks are difficult to study in the wild, and even today little is known of their pair-bonding and social behavior. It is assumed that pair bonds are renewed annually, but few observations exist of courtship and related behaviors. The males certainly do not participate in brood care, and territoriality is evidently weak or even absent, a surprising situation considering that many stream-dwelling ducks are highly territorial.

The females nest in extremely well hidden sites, either on the ground (usually under dense vegetation) or in rocky crevices or other natural cavities. Their eggs reportedly hatch after about 28 or 29 days, but the fledging period is uncertain, with estimates ranging between 40 and 70 days.

Overall population estimates are not available. The Pacific coast population may approach a million birds. The other populations are much smaller.

Thomas Kitchin

Oldsquaw

(Clangula hyemalis)

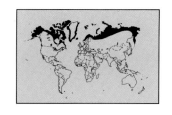

Male Oldsquaw

mostly black, with the flanks remaining white and a white patch developing around the eyes. The female has piebald black and white head markings throughout the year, but its flanks are always grayish white and its breast is always a mottled or scalloped brown. Both sexes have wings that are mostly dark above and below, the secondaries having a brownish sheen in some cases. They are superb divers.

The Oldsquaw breeds on tundra, migrating at times to extremely high arctic latitudes of northern Greenland and arctic Canada to nest. Courtship is a spirited affair, with aerial and aquatic displays. The wild calls of the males carry far over the tundra in one of the most evocative and memorable of all the sounds of the arctic spring.

Females hide their nests in often short vegetation and remain constantly on the nest as they incubate their six or seven eggs for 24 to 26 days. The ducklings grow extremely rapidly, at times fledging in as few as 35 days, which allows the species to breed in areas having only about two months of frost-free weather in summer.

The population is estimated at several million, although detailed estimates are not available.

This attractive sea duck is generally called the Oldsquaw in North America. Ironically, this unfortunate name derives from the loud, raucous calling of the males, not the females. Its British name, Long-tailed Duck, is more appropriate and more descriptive, at least of the male, which has a long, pointed tail much like that of the Northern Pintail. The female, however, has a short tail. Both sexes have an extremely complicated sequence of molts and plumages, making simple descriptions of their appearance almost impossible. Suffice it to say that during the winter the male is mostly white, with a black breast and ear patches, whereas during the summer the head, neck, and breast are

Black Scoter

(Melanitta nigra)

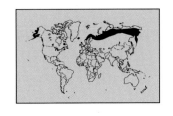

*Male Black Scoter
(Eurasian race)*

The Black Scoter is often called the Common Scoter. Although this duck does have a broad range in northern parts of both the Old and New World, in North America it may be the rarest of the three scoter species. Its more descriptive name, Black Scoter, suits it better: the plumage of the adult male is entirely black. The male also has a distinctive swelling at the base of the bill. The female is mostly dark brown, but its head is two-toned (resembling female Red-crested Pochards), with a darker upper half and lighter lower half. Like all scoters, this bird is mostly found along coastlines, but at times winters on large lakes such

as the Great Lakes. Like other scoters, it forages for various mollusks such as mussels, usually just outside the zone of breaking waves in waters under 25 feet (8 m) deep, and at times may dive to depths of about 40 feet (12 m).

Black Scoters display socially from late winter through spring, with a good deal of aggressive interactions among the participating males evident, and many loud whistling calls uttered by the males, usually just before a vertical tail-snap followed by a low rush through the water toward or past a female. The birds arrive on their arctic tundra breeding grounds rather late, not nesting in Alaska until late June, or about two weeks later than eiders of the same area.

The females often nest under dense shrubby cover and lay clutches of six to nine eggs. Incubation requires 27 to 28 days, and during this time males abandon their mates and usually migrate some distance before starting their post-breeding molts. The fledging period lasts about six to seven weeks, and fall migration begins very soon after the young are able to fly.

This species probably numbers in the low millions. No overall population estimates are available.

Surf Scoter

(Melanitta perspicillata)

Adult Surf Scoters

Like the other two scoters, the Surf Scoter is a fairly common coastal duck along the Atlantic and Pacific shorelines of North America, but unlike the others its range does not extend to Europe and Asia. During winter, it is abundant along rocky coastlines of Alaska and Canada, and young birds or females are occasionally found in freshwater lakes or rivers as well. Like other scoters, the bird forages during much of the year for mollusks, especially mussels, in coastal waters of moderate depth. The adult male can easily be recognized by its white forehead and nape patches that contrast with its otherwise all-black plumage; the female and immature male are mostly dark brown, with darker crowns and small whitish patches on the nape, ear region, and just behind the bill.

Like other scoters, social display in this species is marked by intense competition among the males, with frequent fights and chases, plus several ritualized aggressive postures, and also some short display flights that terminate in skidding stops near the female. A gurgling call accompanies at least one of the displays, which is called breast-scooping, and a chest-lifting posture resembling the rearing display of the Steller's Eider is also performed. Breeding occurs in rather inaccessible brushy habitats near timberline or in heavier woodlands.

Nesting mainly occurs in the interior of northern Canada, but few nests have been found. The incubation period is unknown, as is the fledging period.

No recent overall population estimates are available, though the population probably approaches a million birds.

White-winged Scoter

(Melanitta fusca)

Male White-winged Scoter (North American race)

The White-winged Scoter is easily recognized by its white secondary feathers, which are present in both sexes and all ages. Otherwise, the male is all black, except for its white eyes and a small, somewhat teardrop-shaped patch of white feathers below each eye. The male also has some yellow to reddish markings on its bill. The female is mostly dark brown, and in addition to its white wing speculum has small rounded patches of whitish feathers on the ear region and between the eye and the bill. The species has a broad range in both North America and Eurasia (in Britain it is called the Velvet Scoter) and is perhaps the most abundant worldwide of all scoters. It is the largest and most ponderous of the three scoter species, but like the others, feeds mostly on mollusks in fairly shallow coastal waters.

Courtship occurs at sea during late winter and spring, with much the same sorts of aggressive fighting, chasing, and other male displays that are typical of the other two scoter species. By the time they arrive on their breeding grounds, the females are all paired, but nearly a month may elapse before egg-laying begins. This is in sharp contrast to other arctic-nesting ducks, and the reason for such delayed nesting remains a mystery.

Females deposit clutches of nine or ten eggs in well-hidden nests and incubate them for 27 or 28 days. The young require about 65 to 75 days to attain fledging, which means that fall migration must begin immediately if the birds are to escape the first winter storms.

The population of this scoter probably numbers several hundred thousand birds. No detailed population estimates are available.

Bufflehead

(Bucephala albeola)

Male Bufflehead

The name Bufflehead, which is a contraction of Buffalo-head, seems descriptive of this beautiful little North American duck, which appears to have a head that is too large for its body. In breeding males, the head is magnificently adorned with a triangular white crest bounded in front and below by iridescent tones of green, purple, and bronze. It has at times also been called Spirit Duck, which perfectly catches the essence of this spritc-like creature, whose presence manages to give life to an otherwise empty woodland pond regardless of the bird's minuscule size. Besides the male's white crest, its underparts are also entirely white, and a broad white wing patch is evident in flight. The female is duller than the male but has a small white oval mark behind each eye and a smaller white patch on each wing.

Buffleheads are a delight to watch in any season, but during spring they are entrancing. The males court the females endlessly, in wild aerial chases, aquatic tournaments, and underwater attacks on other males. Somehow the females manage to select mates through all this commotion, and on arrival at their breeding grounds seek out nest sites, often old woodpecker holes. They lay clutches of eight or nine eggs and incubate them for about 30 days. Another 50 to 55 days are required to bring the young to fledging, and at about this time the female begins her own flightless period.

There are probably about half a million breeding birds, which breed mainly in the forests of southern Canada.

Thomas Kitchin

127

Barrow's Goldeneye

(Bucephala islandica)

*Female and male Barrow's
Goldeneyes*

North Americans are indeed lucky to have all three species of *Bucephala* as native species; the two goldeneyes and the Bufflehead are certainly among our most attractive waterfowl species. The Barrow's Goldeneye is mostly limited to the western parts of North America from the Rocky Mountains westward, although a few birds winter along the Atlantic coast as well. The male Barrow's Goldeneye in breeding plumage has a distinctive white crescent between each eye and the bill, and also has a series of white spots extending back along each shoulder. The female greatly resembles the female Common Goldeneye but typically (at least in western populations) has an all-yellow bill and a quite dark brown head with a pronounced forehead bulge. The two species often occur together, and at that time the differences in the females are more readily apparent. This duck forages in fairly deep waters, feeding primarily on mollusks and other invertebrates.

Barrow's Goldeneyes engage in prolonged courtship display during spring, when the loud grunting and clicking calls of the males, as well as their splashing, draw one's attention to them. The males perform a wide variety of displays, but an energetic head-throw-kick is perhaps the most conspicuous of these. Aggressive interactions among the males are also very evident, and indeed many of the male displays seem to have a hostile rather than sexual motivation. In any case, pair bonds are eventually formed, and females begin to seek out nesting sites.

Nests are most often in tree cavities although sometimes in rock crevices; on rare occasions, the birds will nest under dense vegetation. Clutch-sizes number 9 to 11 eggs, and incubation lasts about 32 days. There is a rather long eight-week pre-fledging period, during the late stages of which the female may abandon her brood and begin her own flightless period.

There are probably a few hundred thousand breeding birds.

Common Goldeneye

(Bucephala clangula)

Male Common Goldeneye

Scott Nielsen

The Common Goldeneye is the most widespread and most common of the *Bucephala* species, breeding over large areas of the boreal forests of the Northern Hemisphere and wintering both on coastal waters and larger freshwater lakes and rivers. Indeed, this bird is among the most conspicuous of the diving ducks in many areas, and the nearly all-white body of the male helps to set it apart from most other divers. In breeding plumage, the male has rounded white spots, rather than white crescents, between the eyes and the bill, and a series of black and white diagonal stripes extending back from the shoulders. The female and non-breeding male have chocolate brown heads and mostly gray bodies, and closely resemble Barrow's Goldeneyes. However, the female never has an all-yellow bill, and its head is more triangular (more peaked at the top, rather than flat-topped and bulging at the forehead). Males of either species often court females of the other, making identification somewhat more difficult, and wild hybrids sometimes occur.

Courtship in Common Goldeneyes is marked by an extreme diversity of male displays, which are performed in rapid succession and seemingly in no partic-

ular order. Head-throw displays, with or without accompanying backward kicks, are especially conspicuous, but several other postures are performed. Females initiate these displays with active inciting behavior and eventually solicit copulation from one of the males by stretching out prone on the water. A quite different array of male displays, which is often prolonged, precedes copulation in goldeneyes (and most other sea ducks as well).

Like the other *Bucephala* species, females prefer nesting in cavities, especially tree cavities where they are available. Such sites are often limited, and competition over suitable sites may lead to multiple use and dump-nesting. The usual clutch-size of a single female is about ten eggs, and incubation averages about 30 days. During the brood-rearing period, the young of two or more females often become amalgamated, producing rather large "families" of dependent young.

Overall population estimates are not available, but there are probably more than a million breeding birds.

Hooded Merganser

(Mergus cucullatus)

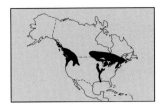

*Female and male
Hooded Mergansers*

Thomas Kitchin

Most observers would probably admit that the Hooded Merganser is among the most visually attractive of all the mergansers; no other duck species is able to alter its appearance so rapidly and spectacularly as can a male Hooded Merganser simply by raising and lowering its crest. This white crest, trimmed and surrounded by black, is in the same place as the Bufflehead's but is far more variable in appearance owing to

its highly erectile nature. It ranges from a rather narrow white stripe (in flying birds) to an enormous white oval that is considerably larger than the rest of the head. The female is also crested, but its crest is mostly rufous brown, and not nearly so varied in shape. Both sexes show a series of slightly curved black-and-white striped tertial feathers on the lower back that cover the flight feathers when swimming or standing. The bill of the

Hooded Merganser is shorter than those of other North American mergansers, but nonetheless is an effective fish-catching device. The birds nest in forested woodlands of eastern and western provinces and states, especially along clear-water streams and tree-lined lakes.

Courtship behavior of the Hooded Merganser is, as might be expected, marked by crest erection, head-shaking, and head-throw displays, all serving to emphasize the large crest. In several ways the species' social behavior is surprisingly like that of the goldeneyes, indicating that these two groups are fairly close relatives in spite of the differences in bill shape.

Females select cavities for nesting, often competing with female goldeneyes or American Wood Ducks for tree cavities, and sometimes even laying eggs in the same cavity. Clutches average about ten eggs, and incubation lasts about 32 or 33 days. Rivers that are rich in small minnows are favored for brood-rearing sites, and about 70 days are needed to bring the young to fledging.

No detailed population estimates are available. There are perhaps close to 100,000 breeding birds.

Smew

(Mergus albellus)

Male Smew

Although European bird-watchers might envy North Americans for their Buffleheads and Hooded Mergansers, the Smew is an equally attractive Eurasian species. On rare occasions, vagrant individuals have reached North America. This species is about the same size as the Hooded Merganser, but, like the Bufflehead, the male in breeding plumage is almost entirely white, with a small black mask from the eyes to the bill. A black V-mark also hangs down from the shaggy nape, and two narrow black stripes are in roughly the same shoulder area where the Hooded Merganser exhibits broad black stripes. The female and immature or non-breeding male have dark chestnut to blackish crowns and faces, contrasting sharply with their white throats and forenecks. The Smew occupies open fresh and marine waters, where it eats not only small fish but also a variety of invertebrate life, including insects, mollusks, and crustaceans. At times it forages cooperatively, diving simultaneously in the manner of some cormorants, thereby probably improving its chances of capturing fish.

Smews display enthusiastically during the late winter and spring months, the males raising their rather short crest, pulling the head back along their shoulders in a bridling movement called pouting, and at times performing a head-fling while uttering the same mechanical rattling call that is used during pouting.

Following pair formation, the females seek out hollow trees, especially broad-leaved species such as oaks, in which to nest. The clutches typically range from six to nine eggs, and at times Smews and Common Goldeneyes have mixed clutches as a result of competition for suitable nesting sites. Incubation lasts 28 days, but little is known of the latter stages of brood-rearing and post-breeding molting patterns.

Overall population estimates are not available. There are perhaps a few hundred thousand breeding birds.

© Wayne Lynch

❧Brazilian Merganser

(Mergus octosetaceus)

This is a little-known species of merganser found in southern Brazil and adjacent northeastern Argentina and eastern Paraguay. Pair-bonding is apparently very strong and permanent in this species, which is unusual for mergansers, and the bird seems to need small, deep rivers with many rapids and waterfalls, much like those used by Torrent Ducks in the Andes. It differs from the Northern Hemisphere mergansers in that the sexes are identical in appearance, with a greenish head, a long and rather shaggy crest, a grayish body, and white wing patches.

The Brazilian Merganser is rare, and at times has been considered extinct. However, it was observed in the Serra da Canastra National Park (Minas Gerais) of Brazil from 1981 to 1985, and was determined to be breeding there. This very small population is more secure than the species as a whole, which may be endangered.

Male Brazilian Merganser

❧Chinese Merganser

(Mergus squamatus)

This merganser of eastern China is sometimes called the Scaly-sided Merganser, in reference to the male's large black scallop-shaped markings on the white flanks in breeding plumage. Otherwise, the male resembles the male Red-breasted Merganser but lacks the brown breast markings and the black and white shoulder patterning. The female more closely approximates the female Common Merganser, having a brown head that is rather distinctly demarcated from the paler and more grayish neck and body colors.

Little is known of the Chinese Merganser's biology and behavior. It breeds in remote areas of northeastern China and eastern Siberia and is largely unstudied. An English ornithologist, David Bell, searched for Chinese Mergansers in the Siberian Sikhote-Alin range during 1990, and reported that the population in that area has declined by more than half in the past two decades. The birds there are limited to stretches of forest-lined river that are now being subjected to heavy clear-cut logging. The logging not only eliminates nesting sites but pollutes the rivers on which the birds depend.

Male Chinese Merganser

Red-breasted Merganser

(Mergus serrator)

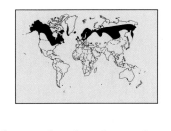

Scott Nielsen

Male Red-breasted Merganser

The Red-breasted Merganser is a medium-sized merganser (its German name, Mittelsager, means "middle-merganser") that is widespread in both North America and Eurasia. It is more prone to winter on salt water than are the Common or Hooded mergansers, and so is more often seen by coastal bird-watchers than those in the continental interior. The male in breeding plumage has a rather shaggy, often double, crest, and a chestnut brown breast with black flecking, as well as black on the back and lower shoulders, plus grayish flanks. The female has a tawny brown head and mostly grayish body; unlike the similar Common Merganser female (and non-breeding or immature males), these colors gradually grade into one another, rather than being sharply separated in the neck region. In both sexes the bill is long and narrow, and generally reddish. Like all mergansers, this bird is very streamlined in flight and is perhaps the most rapid flier of all North American ducks.

Courtship in Red-breasted Mergansers matches the rather wild appearance of the males. It is marked by bizarre neck-stretching and curtsy-like movements that are linked in a rigid sequence called, in German, the Knicks ("bending"). This display is unique to Red-breasted Mergansers.

Once paired, females head for generally forested areas, often near rivers or lakes, and hunt for suitable nest sites in hollow trees or other cavities. Where suitable tree sites are lacking, as in Iceland, the birds typically nest under heavy shrub vegetation. Clutches number nine or ten eggs, and incubation requires 29 to 35 days. The young are reared on small minnows and similar prey and fledge in about 60 days.

There are probably a few hundred thousand breeding birds. Detailed estimates are not available.

Common Merganser

(Mergus merganser)

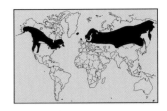

Female and male Common Mergansers

The Common Merganser is generally called the Goosander in Britain, a rather appropriate name in view of the species' large size relative to the other mergansers. The male in breeding plumage is distinctively marked with an all-green head and a body that is mostly white, except for a black back and grayish hindquarters. This white coloration is often tinted with salmon in spring, the color being produced from secretions of the preen gland that are spread over the feathers during preening. The female and non-breeding male not only are substantially larger than Red-breasted Mergansers but their brown heads are also sharply separated from the more grayish body and neck color. They have more definite white chin patches, and their bills are generally heavier toward the base than those of Red-breasted Mergansers.

Common Mergansers spend long periods from late winter through spring in courtship displays. The water splashes made by males during kicking displays at times draw one's attention to displaying birds even when they are too far away for their courtship calls to be heard. Much chasing, diving, and fighting goes on among the males, and distinctive guitar-like notes are uttered by them during vertical neck-stretching, or "salute," displays.

This species nests over large areas of the interior, often along larger rivers or lakes having excellent fish populations. The females prefer to nest in trees, but when such sites are lacking, they will lay their eggs under boulders, under heavy vegetation, or even in abandoned buildings. Clutches average nine or ten eggs, and incubation lasts 60 to 70 days, with the ducklings often forming amalgamated broods before they fledge.

Overall population estimates are not available. There are probably a few hundred thousand breeding birds.

Stiff-tailed Ducks

Guy Fontaine/Ducks Unlimited

Ruddy Duck female and male with ducklings

THE STIFFTAILS ARE A SMALL BUT REMARKABLE GROUP OF DIVING DUCKS OF somewhat uncertain affinities with all the other ducks of the world. There are a few aspects of the Freckled Duck that suggest it might provide a "link" with these waterfowl, and features of the Black-headed Duck (which some people would exclude from the stiff-tailed group) suggest affinities with the dabbling ducks. But such connections appear to be rather weak, and it seems more likely that an early evolutionary divergence of the stifftails must have occurred as these birds became adapted for underwater swimming. This reduced their abilities to walk on land and take off from water. The bill was modified for probing about for insect larvae or other foods found in muddy bottoms: it became especially sensitive to touch and unusually flattened and widened toward its tip.

Most of the species are clearly closely related to one another and can readily be included in the single genus *Oxyura* (meaning "sharp-tail"), but two species are somewhat atypical. One, the Black-headed Duck, is mainly a surface-feeding duck with few external similarities to the typical stifftails, and the other, the Musk Duck, is extraordinarily large with a bill adapted for crushing and swallowing such large prey as crayfish. None of the stifftails exhibit iridescent plumage, but males of nearly all species perform sexual displays marked by tail-cocking, neck-inflation, kicking or other water-splashing behaviors, and sometimes male vocalizations. The latter perhaps helps females or other males detect and localize the presence of territorial males in the sometimes overgrown vegetation where they often occur.

Male and female Black-headed Ducks

The South American Black-headed Duck is not a typical stiff-tail, inasmuch as it lacks a lengthened tail, rarely if ever dives for food, and has a bill shape which more closely resembles that

Black-headed Duck

(Heteronetta atricapilla)

of dabbling ducks. More interestingly, perhaps, it is the only species of waterfowl that is a social parasite; no nest or incubating female of the Black-headed Duck has ever been discovered. It is fairly common on the marshes of northern Argentina, north to southern Brazil, where it is in contact with several other breeding duck species as well as three species of coots. More than a dozen species of birds have been reportedly "parasitized" by Black-headed Ducks. However, the hatching success is very low. Only the fairly short incubation period (about 21 days)

and the precocial condition of the newly hatched young ensure the survival of the ducklings, which are able to fend for themselves when only a few days old.

The number of eggs laid in the course of a breeding season is unknown, although frequently two eggs are deposited in a single host's nest, at about the time that the host female is completing her clutch but before incubation gets under way.

This bird is locally common. No overall population estimates are available.

Female Masked Duck

The smallest and least known of the stifftails is the Masked Duck, which ranges from the West Indies and extreme southern Texas south to southern South

Masked Duck

(Oxyura dominica)

America but is seemingly never common anywhere. Part of its apparent scarcity may be illusory; the birds are easily overlooked among the floating vegetation covering the tropical marshes where they are most common.

The male Masked Duck in breeding plumage has a black facial mask and an otherwise rusty brown plumage. Unlike other stifftails, it has a white wing patch on the secondaries.

The female and immature and non-breeding males have comparable wing markings, but they are heavily streaked with buff and blackish brown on the face.

Nests are usually placed close to deep water in rice clumps or similar vegetation and contain four to six eggs. The incubation period is probably about 28 days, but little is known of the later breeding biology.

No overall population estimates are available.

Ruddy Duck

(Oxyura jamaicensis)

Male Ruddy Duck

The Ruddy Duck is now recognized taxonomically as a species that occurs widely in North America (where the males have entirely white cheeks) but also occurs locally in the South American Andes, from Colombia south to Chile. These Andean forms differ considerably from the North American type. They are substantially larger, and the males have mostly or entirely black heads. Among North American ducks, Ruddys are special in several ways. The male Ruddy is the only North American duck known to have an inflatable neck air-sac (the Masked Duck probably inflates its neck by inflating the esophagus), and the female lays eggs that, proportionate to her weight, are the largest of any North American duck.

Male Ruddy Ducks lack a highly abbreviated late summer eclipse plumage, and instead have a prolonged winter plumage that is carried until the next spring. After their arrival on the breeding grounds, the male Ruddys rather rapidly undergo a pre-breeding molt into their characteristic rusty breeding plumage, and their bills seem to become gradually illuminated from below with bluish neon lighting. By then the males are usually highly territorial, spending much of their daylight hours regularly patrolling the edges of reed beds, with tail erect, neck inflated, and "horns" raised, searching for both females and possible male competitors.

Unlike the half-dozen or so displays of some ducks, the male American Ruddy Duck persistently does one thing, but does it very well. Inflating its air-sac, the male begins a series of progressively faster bill-pumping movements, tapping the underside of its bill on its inflated neck. This not only produces a hollow thumping sound but also forces air from the breast feathers, causing a ring of bubbles to form around the base of the neck. During the bill-pumping sequence, the tail is progressively cocked forward even more, until by the end of the sequence it is almost touching the nape. After the last bill-tap, the male extends its neck forward, opens its bill slightly, and produces a soft belch, perhaps caused by the release of air from the air-sac or esophagus.

This remarkable display is directed toward other males as well as females, indicating that it must serve a dual female-attraction and male-repulsion role. Males also directly threaten and frequently attack other males, occasionally engaging in spirited fights. However, their common response to nearby females is to try to swim directly ahead of them while performing tail-cocking and the "bubbling" sequence.

Nests are built in rather dense reed beds over water that is deep enough for the female to slip away submerged should danger threaten. The water levels must also be fairly stable so that the nest is not flooded or left high and dry. Such ecological situations are now rare, and are mostly limited to the prairie marshes, the northern plains states, and central Canada. About eight eggs are laid, which are incubated for 23 to 26 days. During the rather long fledging period of 52 to 66 days, the young often become separated from their mothers, or simply stray off on their own.

The North American population has averaged more than half a million breeding birds. No information is available on the overall South American population, but the Colombian population is apparently rare.

White-headed Duck

(Oxyura leucocephala)

Male White-headed Duck

Although the North American Ruddy Duck and the Asian White-headed Duck are superficially similar in appearance, earlier judgments that these two stifftails are close relatives were clearly wrong and the result of confused descriptions of male displays. The White-headed Duck is quite distinctive. It has a highly swollen base to its bill and unusually long tail feathers. The adult male has a mostly white head, whereas the female has a very strongly striped face. The body plumage of the male is also less ruddy-tinted and less coarsely patterned than in the other stifftails.

White-headed Ducks spend extended periods in social display and seem to have no actual pair bonds. Instead, dominant males probably control desirable territories and attract females by their display activities. These include tail-cocking and neck-extension displays, as well as a laterally oriented "sideways-hunch" posture accompanied by a mechanical ticking sound, tail vibration, and foot-paddling, all sometimes terminated by a sudden kick. There is also a "sideways-piping" display, also laterally oriented but marked with a double-noted piping call and with accompanying tail-shaking and wing-lifting movements.

Females build their nests in the territories of dominant males and deposit clutches of about seven eggs. Incubation lasts about 25 days, and fledging probably occurs about 60 days after hatching, although actual flight is rare in all stifftails.

The species is now distinctly rare over much of its range, which is centered in the western part of the former USSR, but there is also a tiny remnant population in southern Spain. The more easterly breeding population of the former USSR is migratory, wintering mostly in Turkey. Out of an estimated total world population of about 15,000 birds, the majority are believed to winter on a single Turkish lake, Burdur Gölü. Hunting on this lake was recently banned, and in February of 1990 some 10,900 White-headed Ducks were seen there, establishing the lake's critical value to the survival of this species.

Male Maccoa Duck

The African Maccoa Duck is the only stifftail of that region and is rather similar in shape and behavior to the White-headed Duck. It too has a somewhat swollen bill (these perhaps reflecting unusually large salt

Maccoa Duck

(Oxyura maccoa)

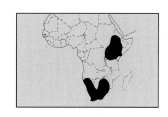

glands that help rid the bird of excess salts in alkaline habitats). The male, however, has an all-black head, and the female is much less contrastingly striped on the face. It is rather widespread in eastern and southern Africa, but seemingly not very common anywhere except perhaps in South Africa. Like other stifftails, it forages by diving, and obtains its food by straining materials from the muddy ooze of pond bottoms.

Dominant males establish well-defined territories along the edges of emergent vegetation, which they regularly patrol and along which they display. Females lay clutches of four to eight eggs, which they incubate for about 25 to 27 days. The fledging period is somewhat uncertain, but the young remain with their mother about five weeks, and may not become fully feathered and completely independent for a few more weeks.

This species is locally common. Overall population estimates are not available.

Argentine Blue-bill

(Oxyura vittata)

Two male and a female Argentine Blue-bill

South America hosts three species of typical stifftails, including the Masked Duck, several races of the Ruddy Duck, and the Argentine Blue-bill, all of which may occasionally come into contact with one another. Generally the Argentine Blue-bill can be recognized by its smaller size, darker plumage coloration (in males), and less heavily streaked faces (in females and young males). This bird favors ponds and marshes rich in emergent vegetation but also having areas of open water for foraging and easy take-offs and landings. It forages at the bottoms of these generally muddy ponds, presumably on insect larvae and the like.

Pair bonds in the Argentine Blue-bill are seemingly rather weak, at least in captive birds, and possibly the same applies in the wild. Clutches of these species seem to be rather small, three to five eggs, and the nests are well hidden in emergent vegetation. Few observations have been made of the nesting and post-nesting phases.

No overall population estimates are available. This species is generally uncommon.

Australian Blue-bill

(Oxyura australis)

Australian Blue-bill female and male with ducklings

The only typical stifftail in Australia is this species, which occurs in much the same areas as the much larger Musk Duck. It closely resembles the Argentine Blue-bill; indeed, males of the two species are difficult to distinguish from one another. Australian Blue-bills have slightly shorter tails and smaller bills than do Argentine Blue-bills, and the facial markings of females do not contrast so much. They both apparently favor permanent cattail-lined marshes for breeding, and forage in mud-bottom ponds for the larvae of midges and similar invertebrates. During the non-breeding season, the bird often inhabits large but shallow lakes, feeding on plant and animal materials.

It is doubtful that pair bonds are formed in this species; instead, the male's ability to establish and defend desirable territory probably plays an important role in regulating individual male reproductive success. Sound-production, using the wings and feet to produce water noises, is a seemingly important part of display, although males also utter very low-frequency calls when performing some postural displays. One of these is sousing, a prolonged series of spasmodic and convulsive movements resembling choking, a seeming climax to a variety of less conspicuous displays. Females appear to pay only scant attention to these displays, and the few copulations that have been documented have followed underwater chases.

Clutches often consist of five or six eggs, which are incubated for 24 to 26 days. The fledging period is evidently protracted, as some 70-day-old ducklings still had their outer primaries encased in sheaths.

This duck is generally uncommon. No overall population estimates are available.

Graeme Chapman/Auscape

Musk Duck

(Biziura lobata)

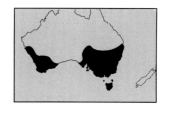

Mark K. Peck

Immature male Musk Duck

It is perhaps fitting that the Musk Duck should be the last duck to be discussed in sequence; it is one of the most remarkable waterfowl in the world, and indeed one of the most amazing of all birds. The male Musk Duck is a large and powerful bird, weighing up to 7 pounds (3 kg). The female weighs about half that. Both sexes are a uniform gray, with long tails and massive tapering bills quite different in shape from those of *Oxyura* species. The adult male produces a strange musky odor of uncertain origin, but probably from the preen gland, and of wholly unknown biological function. The male also develops a large pendant lobe below the bill, which normally hangs down like a loose leather bag but can be enlarged during display. At this time it becomes as large as the head itself, and extends beyond the front of the bill. The Musk Duck is fairly common and widespread in southeastern and southwestern Australia, occurring on swamps, lakes, estuaries, and especially permanent marshes, its prime breeding habitat.

Males differ considerably in size and probably don't reach their maximum size for several years. The largest males establish territories in breeding habitats from which they display almost continuously. Sometimes other, presumably younger, males are also attracted to these displaying males; such males seem to be "onlooker" birds rather than display participants, perhaps being attracted to the accumulated females rather than to the displaying male. The displaying males perform a variety of kicking movements that proceed from simple "paddling kicks" to "whistle kicks." The last is associated with the most intense posturing (tail-cocking, lobe enlargement, and throat inflation), and a sharp whistle accompanies each kick. Evidently pair-bonding is wholly lacking, and after being fertilized, the female goes off to lay her clutch of eggs without further male contact.

The nest is constructed in dense emergent vegetation, and clutches usually consist of only two or three eggs. Incubation lasts about 24 days. The fledging period in wild birds is unknown, but in captivity requires a remarkably long three to four months.

The Musk Duck is generally uncommon. No overall population estimates are available.

Identification Key

The following key provides an efficient means of identifying adults (especially those in breeding plumage) of almost any species of duck in the world if it can be examined fairly closely. The procedure is one of making a series of choices between two opposing descriptive statements (a or b). Simply choose which of the two statements best fits the unknown bird, and follow the indicated numerical pathway of successive choices, with no further regard for the alternative choice. Thus, in the first pair of statements (*1a* and *1b*) you must examine the condition of leg scaling, and then go on to consider a second pair of statements (*2a* and *2b*, or *11a* and *11b*) depending on the scale pattern observed in the unknown bird. Continue to make subsequent choices until you arrive at the name of the unknown species. Although there are 113 pairs of descriptive statements, in no case will more than 15 such choices be needed to identify any of the more than 100 duck species in the key.

Nearly all of the species names in the key are followed by numbers in parentheses, which refer to the numbered head sketches that follow the key and allow for rapid visual confirmation. Comparison with the colored plates earlier in the book is also suggested, especially since only breeding-plumage males are shown in these head sketches, and both sexual and seasonal variations in appearance will exist. Extinct species have been excluded from the key, as have some well-marked subspecies that are sometimes regarded as full species.

Measurements given are lengths from tip of bill to end of tail.

1a	Legs with a network-like scale pattern throughout (whistling ducks and Freckled Duck)	*go to 2*
1b	Legs with a vertically aligned scale pattern in front (all other duck-like waterfowl)	*go to 11*
2a	Legs short; entire plumage speckled with white . . . Freckled Duck **(1)**	
2b	Legs long (extending beyond tail in flight); plumage lacking white speckling (whistling ducks)	*go to 3*
3a	Plumage tawny brown, with a white back . . . White-backed Duck **(2)**	
3b	Varied plumages, but never with a white back	*go to 4*
4a	Legs pink to flesh-colored, bill not uniform gray	*go to 5*

4b	Legs mostly grayish, bill usually gray to blackish	*go to 6*
5a	Pale eyes; long yellow flank plumes . . . Plumed Whistling Duck **(3)**	
5b	Dark eyes, reddish bill . . . Black-bellied Whistling Duck **(4)**	
6a	With white flank spots	*go to 7*
6b	Lacking white flank spots	*go to 8*
7a	Flank spots rounded, surrounded by black . . . Spotted Whistling Duck **(5)**	
7b	Flank spots more irregular, with black edgings . . . Cuban Whistling Duck **(6)**	
8a	Face white, underparts black . . . White-faced Whistling Duck **(7)**	
8b	Face not white, underparts tawny	*go to 9*
9a	14–16 inches (36–40 cm), with yellow eye-ring; wings grayish and chestnut . . . Lesser Whistling Duck **(8)**	
9b	17–21 inches (43–53 cm), no yellow eye-ring; wings brownish	*go to 10*
10a	Underparts pale ochre-yellow . . . Fulvous Whistling Duck **(9)**	
10b	Underparts rich chestnut brown . . . Wandering Whistling Duck **(10)**	
11a	Weakly lobed hind toes, wings usually iridescent (non-diving ducks)	*go to 12*
11b	Hind toe strongly lobed; wings rarely iridescent (steamer ducks and other diving ducks)	*go to 70*
12a	Large (20–30 inches/50–75 cm), with white wing coverts and glossy green speculum (shelducks and Muscovy Duck)	*go to 13*
12b	Size variable, but never with size and wing-color combination of 12a	*go to 19*
13a	Legs pink to flesh-colored	*go to 14*
13b	Legs gray to black	*go to 15*
14a	Head green, bill bright red . . . Northern Shelduck **(11)**	
14b	Head white, bill very pale pink . . . Radjah Shelduck **(12)**	
15a	Plumage almost entirely glossy black, bare skin around eyes . . . Muscovy Duck **(13)**	
15b	Plumage not black; no bare skin around eyes	*go to 16*
16a	Body plumage mostly orange-chestnut; head never green or entirely white	*go to 17*

16b   Body extensively penciled with black; head entirely white or mostly iridescent green

go to 18

17a   Head gray (males) or gray and white (females) . . . Cape Shelduck   **(14)**

17b   Head buff (males) or buff and white (females) . . . Ruddy Shelduck   **(15)**

18a   No white neck-ring; head sometimes entirely white . . . New Zealand Shelduck   **(16)**

18b   White neck-ring . . . Australian Shelduck   **(17)**

19a   Tail long and broad, iridescence of upper wing surface often extensive, underwing often black (perching ducks)   *go to 20*

19b   Tail variable but usually not long and broad; iridescent color almost never present on upper wing coverts; underwing never black (dabbling ducks, Torrent Duck, and Black-headed Duck)

go to 30

20a   Over 26 inches (66 cm), wing coverts white, speculum gray . . . White-winged Wood Duck (very rare)   **(18)**

20b   Usually under 24 inches (60 cm), wing coverts never all white   *go to 21*

21a   Very small (12–14 inches/30–36 cm) (pygmy geese)   *go to 22*

21b   Small (14–24 inches/36–60 cm)   *go to 24*

22a   With brown flanks . . . African Pygmy Goose   **(19)**

22b   Flanks gray or penciled with black   *go to 23*

23a   White of wings mainly on secondaries . . . Cotton Pygmy Goose   **(20)**

23b   White of wings mostly on primaries . . . Green Pygmy Goose   **(21)**

24a   Wing coverts gray to bluish gray   *go to 25*

24b   Secondaries and wing coverts iridescent or at least contrastingly patterned   *go to 26*

25a   Secondaries white, wing coverts gray . . . Australian Wood Duck   **(22)**

25b   Secondaries black; wing coverts bluish . . . Hartlaub's Duck   **(23)**

26a   Head speckled black and white . . . Comb Duck   **(24)**

26b   Head not speckled black and white   *go to 27*

27a   Feet pink or red; 14–16 inches (36–40 cm)

go to 28

27b   Feet mostly yellow; 16–20 inches (40–50 cm)

go to 29

28a   Feet pink, white patch on wing coverts . . . Ringed Teal   **(25)**

28b   Feet red, no white on wing coverts . . . Brazilian Teal   **(26)**

29a   Forehead feather edge V-shaped . . . American Wood Duck   **(27)**

29b   Forehead feather edge rounded or nearly straight . . . Mandarin   **(28)**

30a   No definite wing speculum or other iridescent coloring on plumage   *go to 31*

30b   Distinct, usually iridescent, wing speculum

go to 34

31a   Bill normally shaped   *go to 32*

31b   Bill with soft edge flaps near tip   *go to 33*

32a   Body mottled pale gray . . . Marbled Teal   **(29)**

32b   Body uniformly brownish . . . Black-headed Duck   **(30)**

33a   15–16 inches (38–40 cm), flanks vertically barred . . . Pink-eared Duck   **(31)**

33b   22 inches (56 cm), flanks unbarred . . . Blue Duck   **(32)**

34a   Tail feathers long and stiff, wings spurred . . . Torrent Duck   **(33)**

34b   Tail feathers normal; no wing-spurs   *go to 35*

35a   Wing coverts white, silvery gray, or bluish gray

go to 36

35b   Wing coverts brownish, much like primaries in color   *go to 46*

36a   Wing coverts white or mottled with white   *go to 37*

36b   Wing coverts gray to bluish   *go to 39*

37a   Front of face white; breast scalloped . . . Chiloe Wigeon   **(34)**

37b   Front of face not white; breast not scalloped

go to 38

38a   Underwing coverts and axillaries dark gray . . . Eurasian Wigeon   **(35)**

38b   Underwing coverts and axillaries mostly white . . . American Wigeon   **(36)**

39a   Wing coverts gray (mottled in females)   *go to 40*

39b   Wing coverts bluish gray   *go to 41*

40a   19–20 inches (48–50 cm) . . . Falcated Duck   **(37)**

40b   15–16 inches (38–40 cm) . . . Garganey   **(38)**

41a   Bill of similar width throughout   *go to 42*

41b   Bill shovel-shaped (wider toward tip)   *go to 43*

42a   White facial crescent (males) or small white oval cheek patch (females) . . . Blue-winged Teal   **(39)**

42b   No white on face; bill edges slightly drooping . . . Cinnamon Teal   **(40)**

43a   White breast (males) or orange on bill (females) . . . Northern Shoveler   **(41)**

43b   Breast not white; bill usually blackish   *go to 44*

44a   White facial crescent (males) or grayish brown bill (females) . . . Australasian Shoveler   **(42)**

44b Head uniformly brown and bill black in
both sexes *go to 45*

45a Spotted with black on cinnamon body (males) or
with brown and buff barring (females) . . .
Red Shoveler **(43)**

45b Broadly barred with brown and buff throughout
. . . Cape Shoveler **(44)**

46a Speculum lacking iridescence or nearly so
go to 47

46b Speculum usually iridescent, sometimes blackish
go to 49

47a Speculum mostly buffy, with black anterior
border . . . Red-billed Pintail **(45)**

47b Speculum not mostly buffy *go to 48*

48a Speculum white inwardly and gray or black
outwardly . . . Gadwall **(46)**

48b Speculum blackish, tinted green; buff eye-ring . . .
Brown Teal (rare) **(49)**

49a Speculum with narrow white borders in front and
behind, rear border very narrow or lacking
go to 50

49b Speculum bordered with dark brown to buff in
front, usually broad buff or white border behind
go to 63

50a Speculum green inwardly and black outwardly
go to 51

50b Speculum entirely green, blue, or purplish
go to 55

51a Bill pink, eyes yellow . . . Cape Teal **(47)**

51b Bill not pink; eyes not yellow *go to 52*

52a Eyes brown, anterior speculum border rusty
go to 53

52b Eyes reddish, anterior speculum border white
go to 53

53a Head green (males) or dark brown (females) . . .
Chestnut Teal **(50)**

53b Head light brown, often with white around
eyes. . . Gray Teal **(51)**

54a Speculum bordered in front with black
and white *go to 55*

54b Speculum bordered in front with white only
go to 61

55a Body mostly black, with white barring above . . .
African Black Duck **(52)**

55b Body plumage not as in 55a *go to 56*

56a Bill bluish to grayish blue *go to 57*

56b Bill yellow to olive or orange-red *go to 59*

57a Cheeks uniform rufous; black crown and eye-
stripe . . . Philippine Duck

57b Cheeks streaked; not uniformly pale rufous
go to 58

58a Heavy cheek streaking and dark eye-stripe . . .
Gray Duck (including Pacific Black and
Spot-billed races) **(53)**

58b Finer cheek streaking and narrow eye-stripe . . .
Meller's Duck

59a Bill bright yellow with black ridge . . . Yellow-
billed Duck

59b Bill not as in 59a *go to 60*

60a Body dark blackish brown . . . American Black
Duck **(54)**

60b Body not dark blackish brown . . . Mallard
(including Mottled, Florida, Mexican, Hawaiian,
and Laysan Island races) **(55)**

61a Tail long and pointed, feet yellow . . . Salvadori's
Duck **(56)**

61b Tail short, legs and feet grayish *go to 63*

62a Brown flanks, brown ear-patch . . .
Hottentot Teal **(57)**

62b Gray flanks, no brown ear-patch . . .
Silver Teal **(58)**

63a Outer secondaries blackish, becoming green
inwardly *go to 64*

63b Iridescence covers all of secondaries *go to 66*

64a Head uniformly speckled brownish . . .
Speckled Teal **(48)**

64b Head not uniformly speckled brownish
go to 65

65a Speculum broadly bordered at rear with white . . .
Baikal Teal **(59)**

65b Speculum narrowly edged at rear with white . . .
Green-winged Teal **(60)**

66a Speculum green or blackish green, with broad
buff border behind *go to 67*

66b Speculum bronzy to green, with narrow white
rear border *go to 68*

67a Bill mostly blue; cheeks white . . . White-cheeked
Pintail **(61)**

67b Bill mostly yellow; cheeks brownish . . .
Brown Pintail **(62)**

68a Speculum with buff border in front . . .
Northern Pintail **(63)**

68b Speculum without pale anterior border in front
go to 69

69a White patches on cheeks and neck . . .
Bronze-winged Duck **(64)**

69b No white on cheeks or neck . . .
Crested Duck **(65)**

70a Over 26 inches (66 cm), grayish or brownish with
white wing patches and short, upcurled tails
(steamer ducks) *go to 71*

70b   Under 25 inches (64 cm), slim, tail never upcurled
                                               go to 74

71a   Flightless; primaries nearly hidden when
       wing is folded   *go to 72*

71b   Capable of flight; primaries extending well
       beyond secondaries when wing is folded
       (almost reaching base of tail); tail longer and
       more upcurled . . . Flying Steamer Duck   **(66)**

72a   Limited to Falkland Islands . . . Falkland Flight-
       less Steamer Duck

72b   Widespread on mainland South America
                                                 go to 73

73a   Occurs in Tierra del Fuego to coastal Chile . . .
       Magellanic Flightless Steamer Duck   **(67)**

73b   Occurs in coastal Argentina . . . White-headed
       Flightless Steamer Duck

74a   Tail feathers not long or stiff, legs near
       center of body   *go to 75*

74b   Tail feathers long and stiff, legs near rear of body
       (stiff-tailed ducks)   *go to 107*

75a   Upper wing surface grayish or brownish, with
       white or gray stripe extending from inner secon-
       daries toward primaries; tail short (pochards)
                                                 go to 76

75b   Primaries dark brown or blackish, with white
       limited to secondaries or wing coverts;
       tail sometimes fairly long (sea ducks)   *go to 90*

76a   Bill narrow, bluish or bright red (narrow-billed
       pochards)   *go to 77*

76b   Bill broad, variably concave in outline, never
       pink or red   *go to 79*

77a   Underwing coverts entirely white . . . Red-crested
       Pochard   **(68)**

77b   Anterior underwing coverts gray or blackish
                                                 go to 78

78a   Underwing coverts mottled gray in front,
       becoming white . . . Rosybill   **(69)**

78b   Underwing coverts entirely brownish black . . .
       Southern Pochard   **(70)**

79a   Flight feathers without definite white wing stripe,
       secondaries variably grayish (typical pochards)
                                                 go to 80

79b   Flight feathers with definite white wing stripe
                                                 go to 83

80a   Upper wing coverts dark grayish black . . .
       Ring-necked Duck   **(71)**

80b   Upper wing coverts light to medium gray
                                                 go to 81

81a   Bill long and sloping, entirely dark . . .
       Canvasback   **(72)**

81b   Bill short, with pale band near tip   *go to 82*

82a   Upper wing coverts light gray . . .
       Eurasian Pochard   **(73)**

82b   Upper wing coverts medium gray . . .
       Redhead   **(74)**

83a   Pale band near tip of grayish bill; breast variably
       brownish (white-eyed pochards)   *go to 84*

83b   No pale band near tip of bluish bill; breast dark
       brown to black (scaups)   *go to 87*

84a   Head tinted iridescent green . . . Siberian
       White-eye   **(75)**

84b   Head mostly brown   *go to 85*

85a   Under tail coverts somewhat mottled . . .
       Madagascan White-eye (extremely rare)

85b   Under tail coverts pure white   *go to 86*

86a   Plumage rusty brown; bill dark nearly to tip . . .
       Ferruginous White-eye   **(76)**

86b   Plumage dull brown; bill with pale band near tip
       . . . Australasian White-eye   **(77)**

87a   Head crested (males); under tail coverts white
       (females) . . . Tufted Duck   **(78)**

87b   Head uncrested; under tail coverts dark
                                                 go to 88

88a   Flanks dark brown; no white on head . . .
       New Zealand Scaup   **(79)**

88b   Flanks mostly white (males) or white on cheeks
       (females)   *go to 89*

89a   Bill short and narrow; crown profile high and
       slightly tufted . . . Lesser Scaup   **(80)**

89b   Bill long and broad; crown profile low and
       rounded . . . Greater Scaup   **(81)**

90a   Both wing surfaces and body mostly dark brown
       or black; bill basally enlarged (scoters)   *go to 91*

90b   Wings usually not dark above and below; if so,
       then body distinctly barred or patterned
                                                 go to 93

91a   Secondaries white . . . White-winged Scoter   **(84)**

91b   No white speculum on secondaries   *go to 92*

92a   Forehead feather edges not forming a deep V
       down top of bill . . . Black Scoter   **(82)**

92b   Forehead feather edges forming a deep V down
       top of bill . . . Surf Scoter   **(83)**

93a   White markings on upper wing surface lacking
       or limited to innermost secondaries and a few
       coverts; underwing dark; bill about 1 inch
       (2.5 cm)   *go to 94*

93b   White or pale buff markings on upper wing
       surface; if faint or lacking, the underwing linings
       pale brownish to grayish white; bill usually longer
       than 1 inch (2.5 cm)   *go to 95*

94a   Bill narrow and grayish, with small pale nail . . .
       Harlequin Duck   **(85)**

94b Bill broad basally, with large dark nail . . .
Oldsquaw **(86)**

95a Bill narrow and serrated, with hooked tip
(mergansers)   *go to 96*

95b Bill not narrow, serrated, or hooked   *go to 101*

96a Bill under 1.5 inches (4 cm), total length
15–19 inches (38–48 cm)   *go to 97*

96b Bill over 2 inches (5 cm), total length 19–28
inches (48–70 cm)   *go to 98*

97a White on lower cheeks and anterior wing
coverts . . . Smew **(87)**

97b Lower cheeks and anterior wing coverts not white
. . . Hooded Merganser **(88)**

98a Bill grayish black . . . Brazilian Merganser
(very rare) **(89)**

98b Bill at least partly reddish   *go to 99*

99a Bill very narrow, nostrils located in its basal third
. . . Red-breasted Merganser **(90)**

99b Bill stout, nostrils located near middle   *go to 100*

100a Flanks without scaly black pattern . . . Common
Merganser **(91)**

100b Flanks with scaly black pattern . . . Chinese
Merganser (rare) **(92)**

101a Innermost secondaries straight and tapering,
underwing feathers dark gray (goldeneyes and
Bufflehead)   *go to 102*

101b Innermost secondaries rounded and curved
outward; underwing coverts white to gray (eiders)
                                      go to 104

102a 13–15 inches (33–38 cm), eyes dark . . .
Bufflehead **(93)**

102b 17–19 inches (43–48 cm), eyes light   *go to 103*

103a Forehead sloping, bill with small nail . . .
Common Goldeneye **(95)**

103b Forehead bulging, bill nail large . . . Barrow's
Goldeneye **(94)**

104a Secondaries iridescent purple . . .
Steller's Eider **(96)**

104b Secondaries brown or black   *go to 105*

105a Forehead feathers nearly covering nostrils . . .
Spectacled Eider **(97)**

105b Forehead feathers not approaching nostrils
                                      go to 106

106a Feathering on sides of cheeks forms V that nearly
reaches nostrils . . . Common Eider **(98)**

106b Feathering on sides of cheeks more rounded, not
approaching nostrils . . . King Eider **(99)**

107a Over 24 inches (60 cm), plumage generally
grayish . . . Musk Duck **(100)**

107b Under 20 inches (50 cm), plumage often rusty or
chestnut (typical stifftails)   *go to 108*

108a 12–14 inches (30–36 cm), a white wing patch . . .
Masked Duck **(101)**

108b 14–19 inches (36–48 cm), no white on wings
                                      go to 109

109a Bill noticeably inflated basally   *go to 110*

109b Bill not noticeably inflated basally   *go to 111*

110a Flanks mostly silvery brown, with little barring
evident . . . White-headed Duck **(102)**

110b Flanks either ruddy brown (males) or with
brown and fuscous patterning (females) . . .
Maccoa Duck **(103)**

111a 17–19 inches (43–48 cm), with fairly long bill
and black (males) or obscurely patterned
(females) head . . . Ruddy Duck (Peruvian race)

111b Under 17 inches (43 cm), with shorter bill and
variable head color   *go to 112*

112a Exposed tail slightly longer than bill; females
with obscure facial markings . . . Australian
Blue-bill **(104)**

112b Exposed tail considerably longer than bill;
females with distinct cheek streaking   *go to 113*

113a Cheeks variably white (males) or buff with
somewhat darker streaks (females) . . . Ruddy
Duck **(105)**

113b Cheeks black (males) or whitish with considerably
darker streaks (females) . . . Argentine
Blue-bill **(106)**

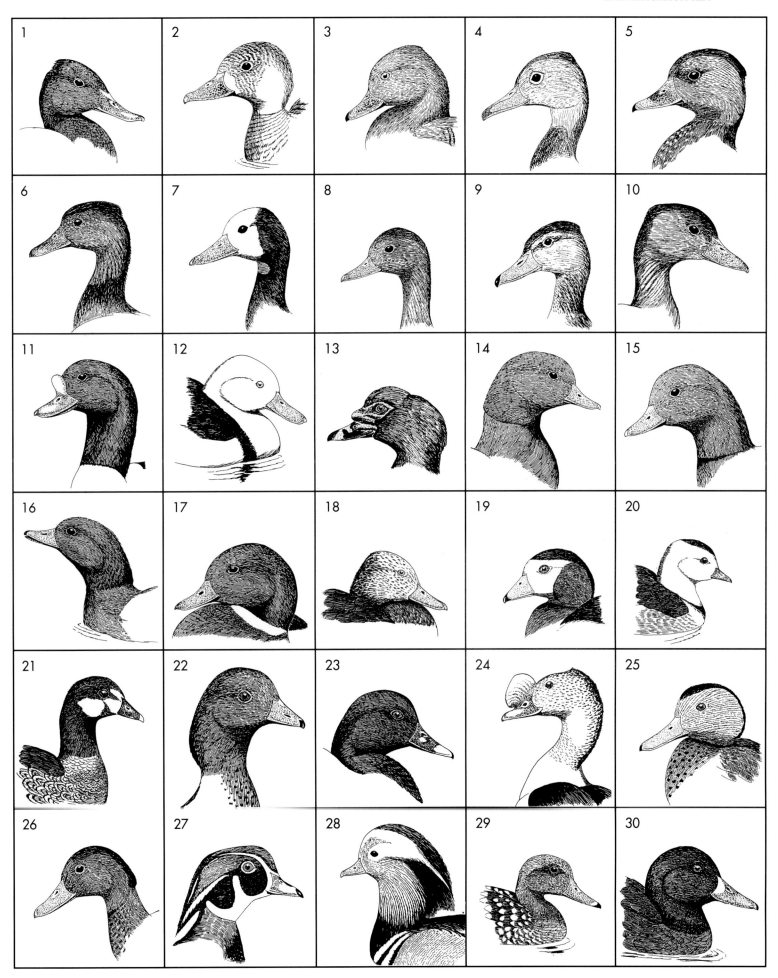

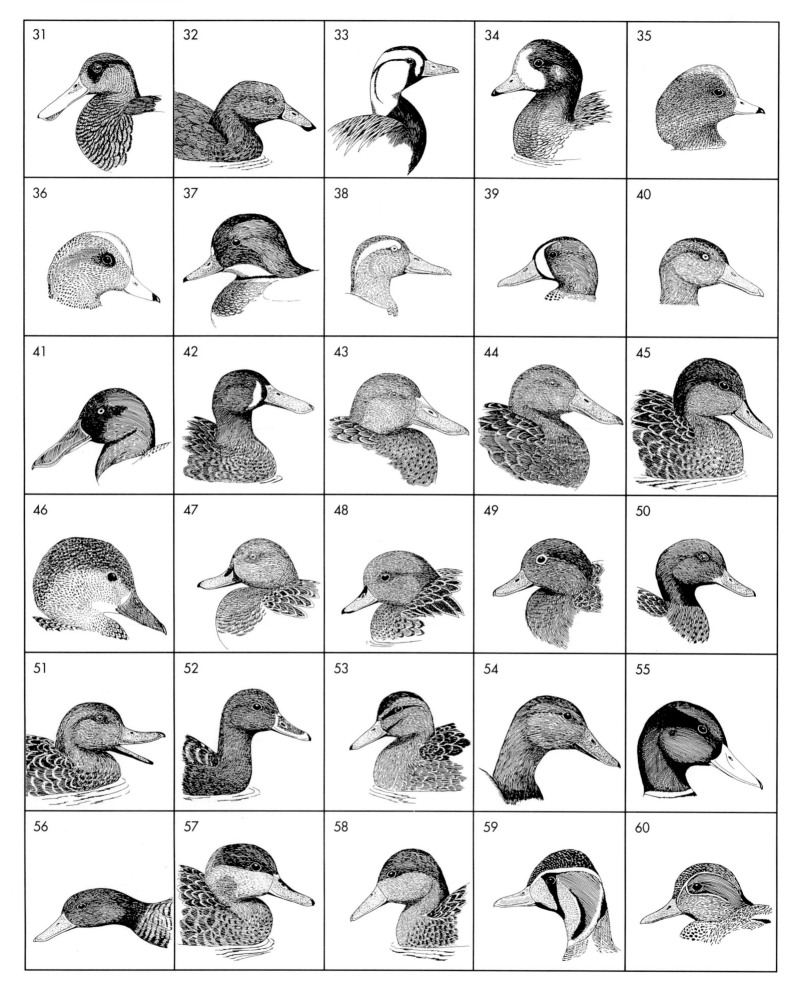

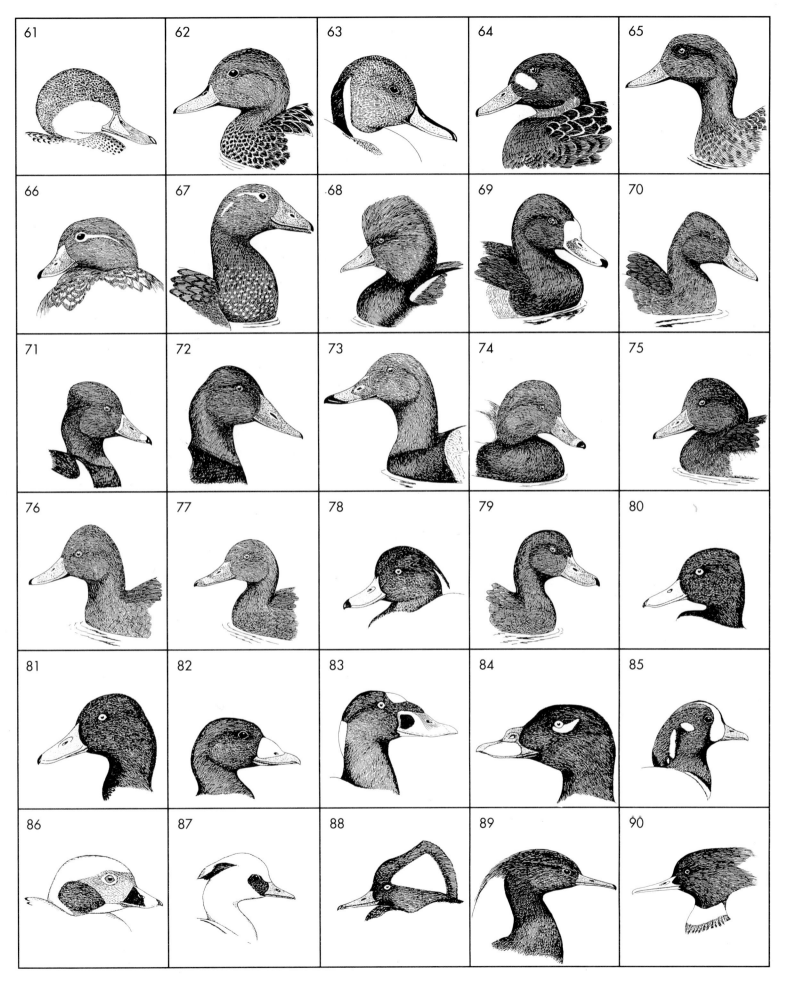

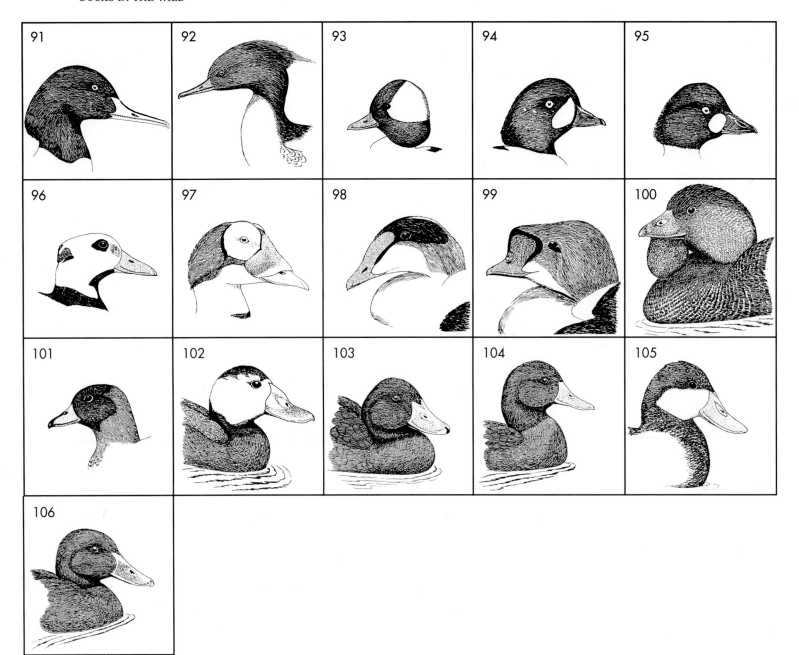

Glossary

Abdomen The underparts, or "belly," of a bird.

Aberrant Diverging from the typical or usual.

Anatidae The taxonomic term for the family of ducks, geese, and swans. The family is further subdivided into subfamilies, tribes, genera, and species.

Anterior Toward the front.

Arboreal Adapted to tree-dwelling.

Austral Southern or southerly.

Axillaries The elongated "armpit" feathers located between the upper flanks and the innermost wing coverts.

Bi-parental care Care and protection of the dependent young by both the male and female; in most ducks only the female provides such care.

Brood To cover and apply heat to hatched young. The featherless "brood patch" of waterfowl is used for transmitting body heat during both incubation and brooding of young.

Bulla An enlarged or inflated bony portion of the syrinx in male ducks, which modifies their vocalizations, often producing whistles. *See also* Syrinx.

Burping A vocalization of male ducks involving whistling while variably stretching the neck.

Caruncle A fleshy enlargement, usually on the head.

Caudal Toward the tail.

Cladistics The determination of evolutionary relationships among a group of related organisms (or clades) by comparing their shared and derived traits.

Clutch A complete set of eggs, normally laid by and also incubated by a single female.

Courtship displays Behavior associated with pair formation and pair bond maintenance, occurring among ducks mainly on the water (social displays) but sometimes also while in flight (courtship flights).

Coverts Small feathers that overlay the larger wing and tail feathers.

Crèche An aggregated "nursery" of ducklings or other young birds, usually tended by one or more adults.

Culmen The upper profile of the bill.

Decrescendo call A vocalization common to most female dabbling ducks, during which the repeated notes diminish in volume and pitch.

Dimorphism Occurring in two distinct forms, such as sexual dimorphism.

Display A means of innate animal communication, often having both visual and acoustic components.

Dorsal Refers to the upperparts.

Double-brooding The attempt to raise a second brood after the successful completion of a nesting in the same breeding season. *See also* Renesting.

Down-up A display of male dabbling ducks in which the bill is first lowered to the water, then is quickly raised, usually with an accompanying call.

Duck A general term for those waterfowl species that are smaller than geese or swans, that mature rather rapidly (in one or sometimes two years), and often exhibit relatively weak pair- and family-bonding behavior.

Duckling A very young duck, typically still partly down-covered and unfledged.

Dump-nesting The laying of eggs by more than one female in a common nest. *See also* Parasitic nesting.

Eclipse plumage A dull, female-like plumage carried by males of many otherwise brightly patterned duck species during the post-breeding season, especially during the flightless period. *See also* Nuptial plumage.

Endangered Existing in such small numbers as to be in danger of extinction.

Estuarine Associated with coastal brackish-water environments.

Extant Still surviving; non-extinct. *See also* Extinct.

Extirpate To eliminate a population locally.

Extinct No longer surviving anywhere in the world. *See also* Extant.

Eye-ring A narrow ring of bare, often colored, skin around the eye.

Falcate Sickle-shaped.

Ferruginous Reddish brown, rust-colored.

Flanks The posterior sides of a bird.

Fledge To take flight for the first time; the fledging period is the period between hatching and fledging. A *fledgling* is a bird that just fledged or is about to fledge.

Flightless period The period during molting when the flight feathers are being replaced, and thus flight is impossible. *See* Molt.

Fulvous Yellowish brown.

Genus The general (generic) name of one or more species of organisms, and consisting of the first part of its scientific name, such as *Anas* or *Aythya*. Unlike the species name, it is always capitalized. *See also* Species.

Goose A general term for those waterfowl species that are usually larger than ducks, forage on terrestrial or aquatic vegetation, and are feathered between their eyes and the base of the bill.

Grunt-whistle A male dabbling duck display involving a quick backward dipping of the bill into the water, followed by a rearing of the body and generally accompanied by a vocalization.

Head-pumping The typical precopulatory display of dabbling ducks, performed mutually by both sexes.

Head-throw A male duck display involving a rapid backward head-toss, usually with an accompanying call.

Head-up-tail-up A male dabbling duck display involving the simultaneous raising of the head and tail, usually with an accompanying vocalization.

Hybrid An offspring individual resulting from the mating of two distinct gene pools, usually separate species.

Immaculate Lacking marks, for example having uniformly white feathers.

Inciting A vocalization and postural display used by females of most duck species to indicate their preferred mate choice, by symbolically "inciting" the favored male to threaten or attack some other individual, often a rival male.

Incubate To apply body heat (or some artificial heat source) to eggs.

Incubation period The interval between the initial application of heat to an egg and its hatching.

Innate Inherited, such as instinctive patterns of behavior.

Instinct A type of inherited behavior that tends to be fairly complex but stereotyped, is dependent on both specific internal states (such as hormone levels) and external stimuli, and provides an innate "language" by which animals can communicate.

Insular Referring to an island or island-like situation.

Iridescence Metallic-colored feathers, resulting from light refraction and reflection that produce rainbow-like colors.

Jump-flight A short and conspicuously noisy flight of a displaying male, usually bringing it closer to a courted female.

Juvenile A young but fledged bird that retains part or all of its juvenal plumage. Juveniles grade into immatures and finally into adults.

Kinked-neck call A male courtship display of pochards, involving a rapid backward bending of the neck while vocalizing.

Lateral Toward either side of the body.

Medial Toward the midpoint of the body.

Migration Fairly regular, often seasonal, movements of an individual or group between two geographic areas, which usually represent breeding and non-breeding (or wintering) grounds.

Mock-preening A ritualized version of preening behavior, occurring during social display. Mock-feeding, mock-drinking, and other similar variations of normal behavior also commonly occur during social display in waterfowl.

Molt (or moult) The process of normal feather loss and replacement in birds. The feathers that are grown during a particular molt cycle represent a seasonal "plumage," such as a nuptial plumage or eclipse plumage. Among ducks, molting typically occurs once or twice a year, depending on the species and the type of feather.

Molt-migration A migration to an area where molting is undertaken, usually performed immediately after breeding.

Monogamy Having a single mate, the pair bond persisting through a single breeding cycle, or indefinitely prolonged.

Nape The back of the head.

Nod-swimming A courtship display involving rapid swimming while lowering and quickly moving the head forward and backward.

Nuptial plumage The generally bright plumage (especially in males) carried by ducks during the pair-forming period, and acquired by molt before breeding. It often alternates with an "eclipse" or "winter" plumage.

Pair bond A variably prolonged and individualized association between an adult male and female that is established sometime before breeding. It may also persist beyond it, encompassing the post-hatching period, when family bonding may occur.

Pair-forming behavior The means by which pair bonds are formed, also known as "courtship behavior." Later, pair-maintaining behavior allows the pair bond to persist as long as may be biologically desirable, which may be for a single breeding cycle or for much longer.

Parasitic nesting The laying of one or more eggs in the nest of another bird of the same or different species, with no later attempt at incubation of these eggs. Sometimes called "egg parasitism" or "social parasitism." *See also* Dump-nesting.

Plumage The collective coat of feathers that is acquired in a molting cycle. *See* Nuptial plumage; Eclipse plumage.

Polygamy Having more than one pair bond during the breeding season.

Posterior Toward the rear.

Precocial Those bird species (including all waterfowl)

whose young are able to feed for themselves and move about easily very soon after hatching.

Primaries The large outer flight feathers ("quills") that insert on the bones of the wing that are beyond the wrist.

Race An alternative general name for a subspecies.

Renesting A nesting effort following a nesting failure during the same breeding season. *See also* Double-brooding.

Reticulated tarsus A pattern of web-like or network-like leg scaling, as opposed to vertically aligned (scutellated) scales.

Ritualized behavior Behavior that has been modified by evolution to serve social communication functions; also known as "displays."

Salt glands Excretory glands located above the eyes that remove excess salts (through the nostrils) in birds that regularly drink salty water.

Scapulars The "shoulder" feathers, located between the median upper wing coverts and the upper back.

Scientific name The Latin (or latinized) name of an organism, typically consisting of two elements (binomial), an initial genus or generic name (which is always capitalized) followed by a species or specific name (never capitalized); for example, *Anas platyrhynchos*. Three-part names are used whenever two or more geographic races (subspecies) of the species are individually recognized. *See also* Genus; Species; Subspecies.

Screamers Semi-aquatic birds of South America that represent the nearest living relatives of the true waterfowl (ducks, geese, and swans).

Scutellated tarsus The somewhat rectangular tarsal plates aligned in a vertical series down the front of the lower leg, as opposed to being more rounded or hexagonal and arranged in a web-like (reticulated) pattern.

Secondaries The major flight feathers ("quills") that insert on the forearm (ulna) of the wing.

Sneak display A male courtship display of pochards, involving the lowering of the head to or toward the water surface while facing another bird and usually calling.

Social display The aquatic and aerial courtship behavior of waterfowl, often involving several males simultaneously displaying to a single female.

Species A "kind" of organism, which exists within a definite distributional range, and normally breeds within its own genetic limits or "gene pool." The term "species" is also used to refer to part of an organism's scientific name. *See* Scientific name.

Speculum The distinctive, often iridescent, color pat-

terns found on the wings of many ducks, usually involving only the secondaries and their coverts but sometimes extending to the primaries.

Subfamily A major taxonomic subdivison of a family. The waterfowl family Anatidae is usually subdivided into three subfamilies, including (1) the Magpie Goose, (2) the swans, true geese, whistling ducks, and Freckled Duck, and (3) all the remaining species.

Subspecies A geographically definable subdivision of a species, also called a "race."

Syrinx The vocal organ of birds, located at the lower end of the trachea.

Taxonomy The science of biological classification of organisms, including the naming of species and higher taxonomic groups.

Territory Specific area defended by an adult or pair, usually during the breeding season, and largely or entirely against others of the same species.

Tertials Inner flight feathers (secondaries) that differ noticeably in shape and/or color from the immediately adjacent secondaries, often being longer and more pointed.

Threatened Species or subspecies that has declined and now exists in small numbers but is not yet regarded as endangered. The term "vulnerable" is sometimes used.

Trachea The windpipe (connecting the mouth and lungs), which in waterfowl includes the sound-producing syrinx.

Tribe A taxonomic category (positioned between the genus and subfamily) that includes one or more related genera.

Tundra Arctic or alpine vegetation occurring beyond or above the treeline.

Turning-the-back-of-the-head A male duck display normally performed in response to female inciting by orienting his nape toward her, an important phase in the pair-bonding process of most ducks.

Ventral Refers to the lower part of the body.

Vernacular name The "common" English name of an organism (usually a species), as opposed to its scientific or Latin name. Standard ornithological usage in North America is to capitalize generally accepted vernacular names of particular species, such as the Eurasian Pochard, but not generalized group names, such as the pochards. *See* Scientific name.

Waterfowl As used here and generally throughout North America, a vernacular term for the family (Anatidae) of ducks, geese, and swans. In Britain, "wildfowl" is used.

Wing-spurs Sharp bony knobs on the anterior wing at its bend or "wrist."

Selected References

GENERAL

Bellrose, F. C. *Ducks, Geese and Swans of North America*. Revised ed. of earlier volume by F. H. Kortright. Harrisburg, Pa.: Stackpole Press and Wildlife Management Institute, 1976.

Brown, L. H., E. K. Urban, and K. Newman (eds.). *The Birds of Africa*. Vol. 1 (Ostrich to Hawks). New York: Academic Press, 1982.

Clancey, P. A. *Gamebirds of Southern Africa*. Cape Town: Purnell & Sons, 1962.

Cramp, S. (ed.). *Handbook of the Birds of Europe, the Middle East and North Africa*. Vol. 1 (Ostrich to Ducks). Oxford: Oxford University Press, 1977.

Delacour, J. *The Waterfowl of the World*. 4 vols. London: Country Life, 1954–64. (Reprinted 1973 by Arco, New York.)

Frith, H. J. *Waterfowl in Australia*. Honolulu: East-West Center Press, 1967.

Gooders, J., and T. Boyer. *Ducks of North America and the Northern Hemisphere*. New York: Facts on File, 1986.

Johnsgard, P. A. *Ducks, Geese and Swans of the World*. Lincoln: University of Nebraska Press, 1978.

——— . *Waterfowl: Their Biology and Natural History*. Lincoln: University of Nebraska Press, 1968.

Kear, J. *Eric Hosking's Wildfowl*. New York: Facts on File, 1985.

Leopold, A. S. *Wildlife of Mexico: the Game Birds and Mammals*. Berkeley: University of California Press, 1959.

Mackenzie, J. P. S. *Waterfowl*. Toronto: Discovery Books/Key Porter, 1988.

Maclean, G. L. *Ducks of Sub-Saharan Africa*. Randburg, S.A.: Acorn Books, 1986.

Madge, S., and H. Burn. *Wildfowl: An Identification Guide to the Ducks, Geese and Swans of the World*. London: Christopher Helm, 1988.

Marchant, S., and P. Higgins (eds.). *Handbook of Australian, New Zealand and Antarctic Birds*. Vol. 1 (Ratites to Ducks). Melbourne: Oxford University Press, 1990.

Ogilvie, M. A. *Ducks of Britain and Europe*. Berkhamsted: T. and A. D. Poyser, 1975.

Owen, M. *Wildfowl of Europe*. London: Macmillan, 1977.

Owen, M., G. L. Atkinson-Willes, and D. G. Salmon. *Wildfowl in Great Britain*. 2nd ed. Cambridge: Cambridge University Press, 1986.

Phillips, J. C. *A Natural History of the Ducks*. 4 vols. Boston and New York: Houghton Mifflin, 1922–26. (Reprinted in 2 vols. 1986 by Dover, New York.)

Scott, P. *A Coloured Key to the Wildfowl of the World*. Rev. ed. Wildfowl Trust, 1988.

Todd, F. S. *Waterfowl: Ducks, Geese and Swans of the World*. San Diego: Seaworld Press, and New York: Harcourt Brace Jovanovich, 1979.

Weller, M. W. *The Island Waterfowl*. Ames: Iowa State University Press, 1980.

WATERFOWL BEHAVIOR

Gauthier, G. "Territorial behaviour, forced copulation and mixed reproductive strategy in ducks." *Wildfowl* 39(1988):102–114.

Johnsgard. P. A. "Behavioral Isolating Mechanisms in the Family Anatidae." In *Proceedings 13th International Ornithology Congress* (C. G. Sibley, ed.), Vol. 1, pp. 531–43. Ithaca, N.Y., 1963.

——— . "Comparative behaviour of the Anatidae and its evolutionary implications." *Wildfowl Trust Annual Report* 11(1960):31–45.

——— . "Evolutionary trends in the behaviour and morphology of the Anatidae." *Wildfowl Trust Annual Report* 13(1962):130–48.

——— . *Handbook of Waterfowl Behavior*. Ithaca, N.Y.: Cornell University Press, 1965.

——— . "Pair-forming mechanisms in *Anas* and related genera." *Ibis* 102(1960):616–18.

——— . "A quantitative study of sexual behavior of Mallards and Black Ducks." *Wilson Bulletin* 72(1960): 13–55.

Kear, J. "The Adaptive Radiation of Parental Care in Waterfowl." In *Social Behaviour in Birds and Mammals: Essays on the Social Ethology of Animals and Man* (J. H. Crook, ed.), pp. 357–92, N.Y. Academic Press, 1970.

Lorenz, K. "Comparative studies on the behaviour of the Anatidae." *Aviculture Magazine* (1951–53), 57:157–82; 58:8–17, 61–72, 86–94, 172–84; 59:24–34, 80–91.

——— . "The evolution of behavior." *Scientific American* 199, no. 6(1958):67–78.

McKinney, F. "The Evolution of Duck Displays." In *Function and Evolution in Behaviour* (G. Baerends, C. Beer, and A. Manning, eds.), pp. 331–57, Oxford: Oxford University Press, 1975.

——— . "Primary and Secondary Male Reproductive Strategies of Dabbling Ducks." In *Avian Monogamy*, P. A. Gowarty and D. W. Mock, eds., pp. 68–82, Washington, D.C.: American Ornithology Union, 1985.

Sharpe, R. S., and P. A. Johnsgard. "Inheritance of behavioral characters in F2 Mallard x Pintail (*Anas platyrhynchos* L. x *A. acuta* L.) hybrids." *Behaviour* 27(1966):259–72.

EXTINCT AND ENDANGERED SPECIES

Ali, S. "The Pink-headed Duck." *Wildfowl Trust Annual Report* 11(1960): 55–60.

Anstey, S. "The status and conservation of the White-headed Duck *Oxyura leucocephala*." IWRB Special Publication 10, 1989.

Boyd, H. "Duck numbers in the USSR, the western Palearctic and North America 1967–86: first comparisons." *Wildfowl* 41(1990):171–75.

Bucknill, J. E. "The disappearance of the Pink-headed Duck." *Ibis*, series 11, no. 6(1924):146–51.

Collar, N. J., and P. Andrew. "Birds to watch: the ICBP world checklist of threatened birds." ICBP Technical Publiction no. 8, 1988.

DiSilvestro, R. "The clouded future of our waterfowl." *Defenders of Wildlife* 64, no. 1(1989):18–29.

Dumbell, G. "The New Zealand Brown Teal: 1845–1985." *Wildfowl* 37(1986):71–87.

Fuller, E. *Extinct Birds*. New York: Facts on File, 1987.

Green, A. "Progress in the White-winged Wood Duck *Cairina scutulata* action plan project: a call for information." *Wildfowl* 41(1990):161–62.

Greenway, J. C. *Extinct and Vanishing Birds of the World*. New York: American Committee for International Wildlife Protection, 1958.

Hayes, F. N., and G. S. Dumbell. "Progress in Brown Teal *Anas a. chlorotis* conservation." *Wildfowl* 40(1989):137–40.

International Union for the Conservation of Nature and Natural Resources. *Directory of Wetlands of International Importance*. Morges, Switzerland, 1984.

Kear, J., and R. Scarlett. "The Auckland Islands Merganser." *Wildfowl* 21(1970):78–86.

Kear, J., and G. Williams. "Waterfowl at risk." *Wildfowl* 29(1978):5–21.

Madson, J. "A lot of trouble and a few triumphs for North American waterfowl." *National Geographic* 166, no. 5(1984):562–99.

Moulton, D. W., and M. W. Weller. "Biology and conservation of the Laysan Duck (*Anas laysanensis*)." *Condor* 86(1984):105–17.

Scott, D. "The Auckland Island Flightless Teal." *Wildfowl* 22(1971):44–45.

Young, H. G., and J. G. Smith. "Notes on an expedition to relocate the Madagascar Pochard *Aythya innotata*—a JWPT, WWF, WWT project." *Wildfowl* 41(1990):159–60.

Warner, R. E. "Recent history and ecology of the Laysan Duck." *Condor* 63(1963):3–23.

WATERFOWL CLASSIFICATION

Brush, A. H. "Waterfowl feather proteins: analysis of use in taxonomic studies." *Journal of Zoology* (London) 179(1976):467–98.

Johnsgard, P. A. "Hybridization in the Anatidae and its taxonomic implications." *Condor* 62(1960):25–33.

——— . "Order Anseriformes." In *Check-list of birds of the world* (E. Mayr and C. W. Cottrell, eds.), vol. 1, 2nd. ed., pp. 425–506. Cambridge, Mass.: Museum of Comparative Zoology, 1979.

——— . "The systematic position of the Marbled Teal." *Bulletin of the British Ornithology Club* 81(1961): 37–43.

——— . "The systematic position of the Ringed Teal." *Bulletin of the British Ornithology Club* 80(1960): 165–67.

——— . "Tracheal anatomy of the Anatidae and its taxonomic significance." *Wildfowl Trust Annual Report* 12(1961):58–69.

Lack, D. *Evolution Illustrated by Waterfowl*. Oxford: Blackwell Scientific, 1974.

Livezey, B. "A phylogenetic analysis and classification of recent dabbling ducks (tribe Anatini) based on comparative morphology." *Auk* 108(1991):471–508.

——— . "A phylogenetic analysis of recent anseriform genera using morphological characters." *Auk* 103(1986):737–54.

Madsen, C. S., K. P. McHugh, and S. R. de Kloet. "A partial classification of waterfowl (Anatidae) based on single-copy DNA." *Auk* 105(1988):452–59.

Sibley, C. G., and B. L. Monroe, Jr. *Distribution and Taxonomy of Birds of the World*. New Haven: Yale University Press, 1990.

Waterfowl Conservation and Habitat Preservation Groups

UNITED STATES

Ducks Unlimited, PO Box 66300, Chicago, IL 60666
A privately funded organization devoted to the conservation and propagation of North American waterfowl, with offices in the United States and Canada. Most of its income is spent on preserving important wetland habitats in central Canada that are major waterfowl production areas. Publishes a popular bimonthly magazine, *Ducks Unlimited*.

National Audubon Society, 950 Third Ave., New York, NY 10022
A privately funded organization concerned with the promotion of conservation and environmental education. Publishes the bimonthly *Audubon*, a general-interest conservation magazine. Also publishes the quarterly *American Birds*, a more technical periodical that documents seasonal bird populations and their distributions in North America, including the results of annual Christmas Bird Counts.

National Wildlife Federation, 1412 16th St. NW, Washington, DC 20036
A privately funded conservation education and lobbying organization. Publishes the bimonthly magazines *National Wildlife*, *International Wildlife*, and *Ranger Rick* as well as a newsletter and various more technical publications related to conservation. Their annual Conservation Directory lists virtually all federal, state, provincial, and privately funded North American organizations concerned with conservation and wildlife management.

Nature Conservancy, 800 Lynn St., Arlington VA 22209
A privately funded corporation devoted to the preservation and acquisition of plants, animals, and natural communities. It has helped preserve more than 5 million acres (2 million ha), including more than 1,200 areas, in the United States and Canada, representing the largest private system of nature preserves in the world. It publishes the bimonthly magazine *Nature Conservancy*.

Ornithological Societies of North America (OSNA), PO Box 1897, Lawrence, KS 66044
This is the inclusive name and collective mailing address for the four largest North American professional and semi-professional ornithological societies—American Ornithologists' Union, Association of Field Ornithologists, Cooper Ornithological Society, and Wilson Ornithological Society—each of which publishes its own technical ornithological journal. The largest of these, the American Ornithologists' Union (AOU), publishes a quarterly ornithological journal, *The Auk*; the others respectively publish quarterlies titled *The Journal of Field Ornithology*, *The Condor*, and *The Wilson Bulletin*.

World Wildlife Fund, 1250 24th St. NW, Washington, DC 20037
The world's largest privately funded conservation organization, headquartered internationally in Switzerland, with 26 affiliated countries. It has supported a wide array of conservation programs on threatened and endangered wildlife and their habitats in more than 100 countries, and has published or assisted in the publication of various books and reports on endangered species and related research.

CANADA

Canadian Nature Federation, 453 Sussex Drive, Ottawa, Ont. K1N 6Z4
A privately funded organization devoted to educating the public about the ecological aspects of managing natural resources. Publishes the magazine *Nature Canada*.

Ducks Unlimited (Canada), 1190 Waverley St., Winnipeg, Man. R3T 2EZ
Publishes the quarterly magazine *The Conservator*. See U.S. description above.

Nature Conservancy of Canada, Suite 611, 2200 Yonge St., Toronto M4S 2E1
A privately funded organization devoted to the acquisition and protection of natural areas throughout Canada. See U.S. description above.

GREAT BRITAIN

British Trust for Ornithology (BTO), The Nunnery, Nunnery Place, Thetford, Norfolk IP24 2PU
Collects and organizes bird distribution and abundance data for Britain, and publishes the journals *Bird Study* and *Ringing and Migration*.

International Council for Bird Preservation (ICBP), 32 Cambridge Rd., Girton, Cambridge CB3 OPJ

An international confederation of more than 300 bird-conservation societies representing more than 100 countries. Supports global research on bird conservation, and publishes a quarterly journal, *Bird Conservation International*, plus a variety of technical reports and monographs.

Royal Society for the Protection of Birds (RSPB), The Lodge, Sandy, Bedfordshire SG19 2DL

Britain's largest privately funded conservation organization (with more than 500,000 members). Generally concerned with nature protection, habitat preservation, and environmental conservation, both in Britain and internationally; it supports conservation projects in more than 20 countries. It also manages over 100 nature reserves, totaling more than 250,000 acres (40 000 ha). Publishes the *RSPB Conservation Review* and the more popularly oriented magazine *Birds*.

The Wildfowl and Wetlands Trust, Slimbridge, Gloucestershire GL2 1BR

A privately funded organization that performs international research on waterfowl and wetlands, and maintains several collections of living waterfowl (Anatidae) for captive breeding and for educational as well as basic and applied research purposes. Also manages several natural areas that are important habitats for British waterfowl. Publishes an annual report, *Wildfowl*, of collected scientific reports on waterfowl and wetlands and their conservation, as well as *Wildfowl World*, a more popular semi-annual magazine. The trust also houses the Secretariat of the International Waterfowl and Wetlands Research Bureau (IWRB), a waterfowl-oriented offshoot of the ICBP (see above).

EUROPE

International Union for Conservation of Nature and Natural Resources (IUCN), 1110 Morges, Switzerland

An independent body of scientists devoted to promoting the scientific management and preservation of global natural resources. Publishes a wide variety of reports, bulletins, and research monographs.

Lega Italiana Protezione Uccelli, Vicolo San Tiburzio 5, 431 Parma, Italy

Italy's national bird protection organization.

Ligua Para a Proteccao de Natureza, Estrado do Calhariz de Benfica 187, 1500 Lisbon, Portugal

Portugal's national nature protection organization.

Ligue Française pour la Protection des Oiseaux, La Corderie Royale, BP263, F-17315 Rochefort, France

France's national bird protection organization.

Ligue Royale Belge pour la Protection des Oiseaux, rue Royal Ste-Marie 105, 1030 Brussels, Belgium

Belgium's national bird protection organization.

Naturschutzbund Deutschland, Am Michaelshof 8-10, 5300 Bonn 2, Germany

Germany's national nature protection organization.

Nederlandse Verleniging tot Bescherming van Vogels, Drieberseweg 16c, 3708-ZLB Zeist, Netherlands

Holland's national bird protection organization.

Société Romande pour l'Étude et la Protection des Oiseaux, PO Box 54, 1197 Prangins, Switzerland

Switzerland's national bird protection organization.

AFRICA

Southern African Ornithological Society (SAOS), PO Box 87234, Houghton, Johannesburg 2041, South Africa

Africa's largest ornithological organization. Publishes the technical journal *Ostrich*, and the more popularly oriented *Birding in Southern Africa*.

AUSTRALIA AND NEW ZEALAND

Royal Australasian Ornithologists Union (RAOU), 21 Gladstone St., Moonee Ponds, Victoria 3039, Australia

Australia's largest ornithological society. Publishes the journal *The Emu* and the *RAOU Newsletter*.

Royal Forest and Bird Protection Society of New Zealand, PO Box 631, Wellington, New Zealand

Publishes the journal *Notornis*.

Index of Vernacular and Scientific Names